ATLAS OF MY WORLD

First published by Parragon in 2012

Parragon
Queen Street House
4 Queen Street
Bath BA1 1HE, UK
www.parragon.com

ISBN 978-1-4454-9334-3

Printed in China

Discovery KIDS™

ATLAS OF MY WORLD

PaRragon

Bath · New York · Singapore · Hong Kong · Cologne · Delhi
Melbourne · Amsterdam · Johannesburg · Shenzhen

CONTENTS

THE AMERICAS

ASIA

OCEANIA

AFRICA

THE WORLD IN FIGURES

INTRODUCTION

Our planet is an amazing place!

Its seas and oceans are full of incredible plants and animals, from tiny coral to enormous whales.

On land, the scenery ranges from scorching deserts and fertile plains to soaring mountains. These fantastic features have been formed over millions of years by the powerful forces of plate tectonics and the continual action of wind, rain, ice, snow, and heat.

This book will take you on an amazing journey through the continents, showing the natural features found in each of them. It will also reveal who lives there and some of the wonderful sites created by humankind.

There is a helpful glossary on pages 218–219 and you will find these words in **bold** in the main text.

TROPICAL PARADISE
THIS CORAL ATOLL, SURROUNDED BY A SHALLOW LAGOON, SHOWS ONE OF THE CHAIN OF 1300 SMALL ISLANDS THAT MAKE UP THE MALDIVES.

THE WORLD
INTRODUCTION

The Earth is a unique place in our solar
system. It is the only planet we know of where
life exists. Its surface is teeming with plants
and creatures who live in a wide range of
habitats. Also living on this planet are more
than 7 billion people, who are packed into
busy cities or rural settlements.

Deep beneath the Earth's surface, powerful
forces push and pull on the thin crust above.
These forces can split the land apart causing
powerful earthquakes and volcanic eruptions.
At the same time, they can send landmasses
crashing into each other and push mountains
high into the air.

A THICK ICE SHEET
GREENLAND IS COVERED BY A THICK ICE SHEET IN THIS IMAGE TAKEN BY A
SATELLITE IN ORBIT HIGH ABOVE THE EARTH.

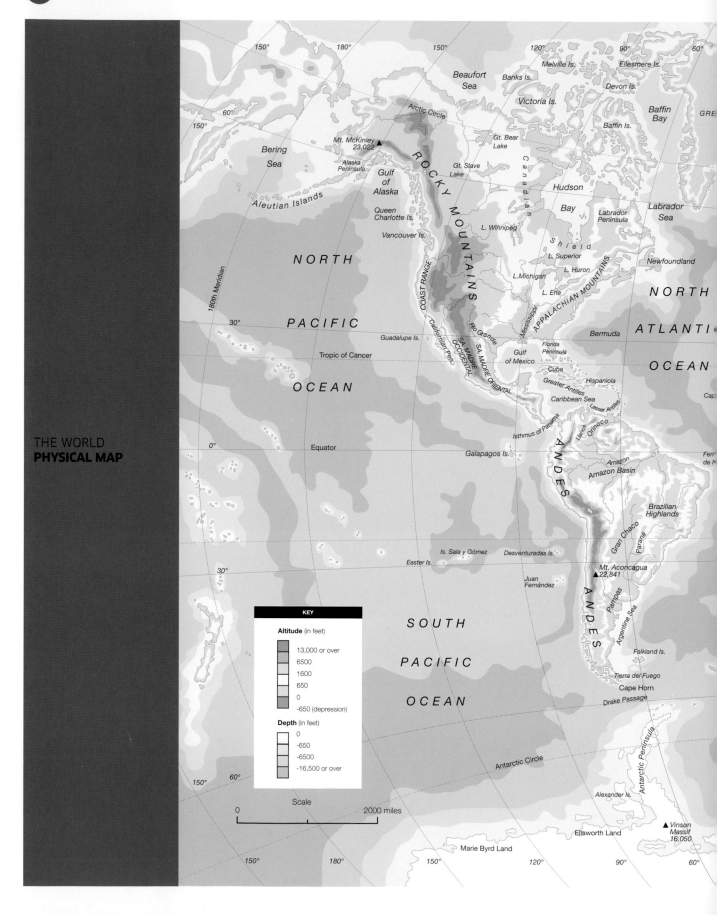

THE WORLD
PHYSICAL MAP

150°   180°   150°   120°   90°   60°

Melville Is.   Ellesmere Is.
Beaufort   Banks Is.   Devon Is.
Sea   Victoria Is.   Baffin
Bay   GRE
60°   Arctic Circle   Baffin Is.
150°   Gt. Bear   Lake
Mt. McKinley   Lake
23,022
Bering   Alaska   Gt. Slave   Hudson   Labrador
Sea   Peninsula   Lake   Bay   Labrador   Sea
Gulf   Peninsula
of   L. Winnipeg
Aleutian Islands   Alaska   Shield   Newfoundland
Queen   L. Superior
Charlotte Is.   L. Michigan   L. Huron   NORTH
Vancouver Is.   L. Erie
NORTH   ATLANTIC
180th Meridian   Bermuda   OCEAN
30°   Guadalupe Is.   Florida   Peninsula
PACIFIC   Tropic of Cancer   Gulf   Cuba
of Mexico   Hispaniola
Greater Antilles   Cap
OCEAN   Caribbean Sea   Lesser Antilles
Isthmus of Panama   Orinoco
0°   Equator   Galapagos Is.   Ferr
de N
Amazon   Amazon Basin
Brazilian
Highlands
Is. Sala y Gómez   Desventuradas Is.   Gran Chaco   Paraná
Easter Is.   Mt. Aconcagua
30°   22,841
Juan   Pampas
Fernández   Argentine Sea   Falkland Is.

SOUTH   Tierra del Fuego
Cape Horn
PACIFIC   Drake Passage

OCEAN   Antarctic Peninsula

Antarctic Circle

150°   60°   Alexander Is.

150°   Scale   Vinson
0   2000 miles   Ellsworth Land   Massif
16,050
150°   180°   150°   Marie Byrd Land   120°   90°   60°

KEY

Altitude (in feet)

13,000 or over
6500
1600
650
0
-650 (depression)

Depth (in feet)

0
-650
-6500
-16,500 or over

COAST RANGE   ROCKY MOUNTAINS   Canadian   APPALACHIAN MOUNTAINS
Rio Grande   Mississippi
SA. MADRE OCCIDENTAL   SA. MADRE ORIENTAL   Llanos
ANDES   ANDES   ANDES

ARCTIC OCEAN

Svalbard

Jan Mayen Is.

North Cape

Novaya Zemlya

Barents Sea

New Siberian Islands

North Siberian Lowland

Arctic Circle

150°

60°

Kola Peninsula

SCANDINAVIAN MOUNTAINS

Norwegian Sea

Baltic Sea

L. Onega

East European Plain

North Sea

British Isles

North European Plain

Central Russian Upland

URAL MOUNTAINS

Ob

West Siberian Plain

Central Siberian Plateau

Lena

KOLYMA MOUNTAINS

Bering Sea

Kamchatka Peninsula

Aleutian Islands

ALPS

Mt. Blanc 15,781

APENNINES

BALKANS

Danube

Black Sea

CAUCASUS

Caspian Sea

Aral Sea

TIEN SHAN

L. Baikal

Volga

ALTAI MOUNTAINS

YABLONOVYY MOUNTAINS

Amur

Sea of Okhotsk

Sakhalin

Hokkaido

NORTH

Iberian Peninsula

Mediterranean Sea

Anatolian Plateau

Mt. Elbrus 18,510

Syrian Desert

Iranian Plateau

TIBETAN PLATEAU

Plateau of Mongolia

Huang He

Sea of Japan

Honshu

Mt. Fuji 12,388

PACIFIC

Crete

ATLAS MOUNTAINS

Libyan Desert

Persian Gulf

HIMALAYAS

Mt. Everest 29,030

Yangtse

East China Sea

Kyushu

30°

SAHARA

Tiger

L. Chad

Nile

Red Sea

Arabian Peninsula

Indus

Ganges

Deccan Plateau

Western Ghats

Eastern Ghats

Bay of Bengal

Andaman Is.

Indochinese Peninsula

Hainan

South China Sea

Luzon

Philippine Sea

OCEAN

Tropic of Cancer

Arabian Sea

Ethiopian Highlands

Socotra

Somali Peninsula

Lakshadweep Is.

Maldive Is.

Sri Lanka

Nicobar Is.

Mindanao

Gulf of Guinea

Congo

Congo Basin

L. Victoria

Mt. Kilimanjaro 19,340

L. Tanganyika

L. Malawi

Sumatra

Borneo

Sulawesi

Java

Flores

Timor

Puncak Jaya 16,500

New Guinea

Equator

0°

Namib Desert

Kalahari Desert

Madagascar

Mozambique Channel

INDIAN

OCEAN

Coral Sea

The Great Divide

Great Barrier Reef

Great Sandy Desert

Simpson Desert

Tropic of Capricorn

SOUTH

Cape Agulhas

Great Victoria Desert

Darling

30°

Mt. Kosciusko 7310

North Island

ATLANTIC

Tasmania

New Zealand

South Island

OCEAN

SOUTH

PACIFIC

Greenwich Meridian

60°

OCEAN

Wilkes Land

Antarctic Circle

150°

Queen Maud Land

0°   30°   60°   90°   120°   150°   180°   150°

ARCTIC OCEAN

Svalbard
(Norway)

New Siberian Is.

ALASKA
(USA)

Arctic Circle

Novaya
Zemlya

Jan Mayen Is.
(Norway)

R U S S I A

Aleutian Islands (USA)

Sakhalin

NORWAY
SWEDEN
FINLAND

Helsinki
Oslo
Stockholm
Tallinn
ESTONIA
Riga
LATVIA
Moscow

Astana

Hokkaido

N O R T H

DENMARK
Copenhagen
Berlin
Amsterdam
NETHERLANDS
GERMANY
Warsaw
POLAND
Minsk
BELARUS
Kiev
UKRAINE

MONGOLIA
Ulan Bator

NORTH
KOREA
Pyongyang
Honshu
JAPAN
Tokyo

P A C I F I C

UNITED
KINGDOM
Dublin
London
IRELAND
Brussels
BELGIUM
Paris
FRANCE
Bern
SWITZERLAND

KAZAKHSTAN

Beijing

SOUTH
KOREA
Seoul

Astana
Bishkek
KYRGYZSTAN
Tashkent
UZBEKISTAN

CHINA

Ryukyu Is.
30°

PORTUGAL
SPAIN
Lisbon
Madrid
Balearic Is.
(Spain)
Rabat
MOROCCO

MONACO
Corsica
(France)
Sardinia
ITALY
Rome
Sicily
TUNISIA
Tunis
Algiers
Valletta
MALTA
Crete

VIENNA
AUSTRIA
HUNGARY
Budapest
ROMANIA
SERBIA
Bucharest
BULGARIA
Sofia
Belgrade
Tirana
GREECE
Athens
TURKEY
Ankara

GEORGIA
Tbilisi
ARMENIA
Yerevan
AZERBAIJAN
Baku
TURKMENISTAN
Ashgabat
TAJIKISTAN
Dushanbe

Tropic of Cancer

OCEAN

Kabul
Islamabad
Taipei
TAIWAN

NICOSIA
CYPRUS
LEBANON
Beirut
SYRIA
Damascus
ISRAEL
Jerusalem
JORDAN
Amman

IRAQ
Baghdad
Tehran
IRAN
AFGHANISTAN
PAKISTAN

New Delhi
NEPAL
Kathmandu
Thimphu
BHUTAN
BANGLADESH
Dhaka

Hanoi
Luzon
Manila

ALGERIA
LIBYA
EGYPT
Cairo

SAUDI
ARABIA
Riyadh
KUWAIT
Kuwait City
QATAR
Doha
UNITED
ARAB
EMIRATES
Abu Dhabi
Muscat
OMAN

MYANMAR
(BURMA)
Yangon
LAOS
Vientiane
THAILAND
Bangkok
VIETNAM

INDIA

PHILIPPINES

Mindanao

PALAU
Koror

MAURITANIA
Nouakchott
MALI
NIGER
CHAD
Khartoum
SUDAN
ERITREA
Asmara
YEMEN
Sana
ETHIOPIA
Addis Ababa
DJIBOUTI
Djibouti

Lakshadweep Is.
(India)
Socotra
(Yemen)

Andaman
Is.
(India)

CAMBODIA
Phnom Penh

BRUNEI
Bandar Seri Begawan

SENEGAL
Bamako
BURKINA
FASO
Ouagadougou
Niamey
N'Djamena
CENTRAL
AFRICAN REP.
Bangui
SOUTH
SUDAN

SRI LANKA
Kotte
Nicobar
Is.
(India)
MALDIVES
Malé

MALAYSIA

GUINEA
SIERRA
LEONE
CÔTE
D'IVOIRE
Abidjan
Accra
GHANA
Lomé
Porto Novo
NIGERIA
Abuja
CAMEROON
Yaoundé

UGANDA
Kampala
Kigali
RWANDA
Bujumbura
BURUNDI
SOMALIA
Mogadishu

KUALA LUMPUR
SINGAPORE

Borneo

Sulawesi

NAURU

LIBERIA
EQUATORIAL GUINEA
Malabo
SÃO TOMÉ
& PRÍNCIPE
Libreville
GABON
CONGO
Brazzaville
Kinshasa
DEMOCRATIC
REPUBLIC
OF THE
CONGO

Nairobi
KENYA
TANZANIA
Dodoma
Luanda

SEYCHELLES
Victoria

I N D O N E S I A
Jakarta

PAPUA
NEW GUINEA
Port Moresby

SOLOMON
ISLANDS
Honiara

TUVALU

ANGOLA
ZAMBIA
Lusaka
Lilongwe
MALAWI

COMOROS
Moroni

VANUATU
Port Vila

NEW
CALEDONIA
Nouméa

FIJI
Suva

NAMIBIA
Windhoek
BOTSWANA
Gaborone
ZIMBABWE
Harare
MOZAMBIQUE
MADAGASCAR
Antananarivo

Port Louis
MAURITIUS

Réunion
(France)

I N D I A N

Greenwich Meridian

SOUTH
AFRICA
Cape Town
Pretoria
Mbabane
SWAZILAND
Maputo
Maseru
LESOTHO

O C E A N

Tropic of Capricorn

AUSTRALIA

30°

S O U T H

A T L A N T I C

Canberra

NEW
ZEALAND
Wellington

O C E A N

	COUNTRY	CAPITAL
1	MACEDONIA	Skopje
2	MONTENEGRO	Podgorica
3	BOSNIA HERZEGOVINA	Sarajevo
4	CROATIA	Zagreb
5	SLOVENIA	Ljubljana
6	SAN MARINO	San Marino
7	LIECHTENSTEIN	Vaduz
8	LUXEMBOURG	Luxembourg
9	ANDORRA	Andorra la Vella
10	KOSOVO	Pristina
11	BAHRAIN	Manama

S O U T H

P A C I F I C

O C E A N

A N T A R C T I C A

Antarctic Circle

60°

THE EARTH'S MOVEMENTS

Like all the planets in the solar system, the Earth spins on its own axis and it also orbits the Sun. These two movements cause the difference between day and night and the changing of the seasons.

23.5°
The angle at which the Earth is tilted.

20/21 JUNE
The longest day in the northern hemisphere happens on the summer solstice.

Yearly Orbit
The Earth takes 365 days, 5 hours, and 48 minutes to orbit the Sun. As the Earth changes position, the seasons and the length of the day and night change, too. The winter solstice is the shortest day of the year, while the summer solstice is the longest day. At the equinoxes, day and night are of equal length all over the planet.

(NOT TO SCALE)

SUN

22/23 SEPTEMBER
This is the autumn equinox in the northern hemisphere. Day and night are both 12 hours long.

91.7 MILLION MILES

Axis of rotation

21/22 DECEMBER
This is the winter solstice in the northern hemisphere. It is the shortest day of the year.

Daily Rotation
The Earth turns around its own axis each day. This movement causes day and night. It also makes the planet slightly flattened at the poles and causes ocean currents.

94.8 MILLION MILES

20/21 MARCH
This is the spring
equinox in the
northern hemisphere.
Day and night are the
same length.

Hemispheres

The Earth is divided into two
halves, or hemispheres:
the northern hemisphere and
the southern hemisphere. The
equator is the imaginary line
that separates them. When it
is summer in the north, it is
winter in the south.

Northern
Hemisphere

Equator

Southern
Hemisphere

LEAP YEAR
Every fourth year,
the month of
February has
29 days instead
of 28. This is
called a leap year.

Jet lag
Long-distance flights can cause
jet lag. This is because a change
in time zones can upset our
body's natural rhythm.

Time Zones

The Earth is divided into 24 different
time zones by imaginary lines that go
from pole to pole. Each zone's time is one
hour different from its neighbors, with the
Greenwich Meridian at the center.

GREENWICH
MERIDIAN

24:00
HOURS

West   East

3:00   21:00

6:00   18:00

N

9:00   15:00

12:00
HOURS

STRUCTURE OF THE EARTH

The Earth is very different under its surface. The rocky ground on which we live is only a thin crust. Underneath the crust is the mantle, made of solid and liquid rock, and in the center is a hot metal core. The whole planet is surrounded by a layer of gases that form the atmosphere.

How Far Have We Explored?

It is more than 3728 miles from the surface to the center of the Earth. So far, we have managed to explore 7.5 miles down.

Mount Everest 5.5 mi

Drilling on land

Drilling under the ocean

1.2 mi

7.5 mi

(NOT TO SCALE)

ATMOSPHERE 1243 MI

THE EARTH 3958 MI

Outer mantle
The movement of the outer mantle causes earthquakes and volcanoes.

385 MI

1398 MI

1392 MI

Inner core
The inner core is made of solid iron and **nickel**.

Outer core
The outer core is made of molten iron and nickel.

Inner mantle
Heavy rocks make up the mantle. They have a temperature of more than 1832 °F.

HOT PLANET
The temperature
of the Earth rises
the closer you get
to the center.

THERMOSPHERE

MESOSPHERE

STRATOSPHERE

TROPOSPHERE

The Atmosphere

**The atmosphere is made
up of a mixture of gases,
mainly nitrogen and
oxygen. It is divided
into different layers
depending on the amount
of gases at each height.
The atmosphere gives us
the air we breathe, and
it protects us from the
Sun's harmful rays.**

Crust
This outer
layer of rock is
4–43 miles thick.

Solar
radiation

Solar
radiation

No atmosphere
Without an
atmosphere, life would
be wiped out by the
radiation and heat.

Atmosphere
Filters the Sun's
rays and distributes
its heat.

The Hydrosphere

**The hydrosphere is the name for the
liquid part of the Earth, including the
oceans, lakes, rivers, groundwater,**

**and water in the atmosphere. Water
covers more than two-thirds of the
Earth's surface.**

LAND OR OCEAN?

TOTAL VOLUME OF WATER

FRESH WATER

29.2%
land

70.8%
water

97%
salt

3%
fresh

2.15%
groundwater

0.85% ice

0.01%
surface and
atmosphere

THE EARTH'S CRUST

The continents and oceans are found on the Earth's crust. This crust is made up of huge pieces that fit together like a jigsaw puzzle. They are called tectonic plates. These plates float on molten rock, or magma.

NEW ROCKS
When magma from a volcano cools, it forms new rocks in the Earth's crust.

Shaping the Earth's Crust

1 Folds
When two plates push together, they form folds. These folds are seen on the surface of the crust as mountains. The Alps, Andes, and Rockies are examples of **fold mountains**.

2 Ridges
When two tectonic plates move apart, they leave a gap. This gap is filled with magma from inside the Earth. The magma hardens to form a ridge.

Continental drift
The tectonic plates are continually moving and can move as much as 4 inches each year. This movement is called **continental drift**.

Tonga Trench

East Pacific Rise

Nazca Plate

Indo-Australian Plate

Moving magma
Underneath the crust, the molten magma is constantly moving. Hotter magma rises, while cooler magma sinks. The moving magma drags along the tectonic plates, causing them to move.

43 miles

The maximum thickness of the Earth's crust.

Fault Lines

The plates in the Earth's crust are separated along cracks called fault lines. The rock along a fault can move suddenly. When this happens, we feel the movement as an earthquake.

Tectonic Plates

The Earth's crust is made up of seven major tectonic plates plus several smaller ones.

The tectonic plates around North America

South American Plate

Mid-Atlantic Ridge

African Plate

Continental crust

THE OCEANS AND SEAS

Much of the Earth is covered by a large body of salt water, which surrounds the continents. The water forms large, deep oceans and smaller, shallow seas. Underneath the waves, there are huge underwater mountain ranges called ridges and deep valleys called trenches.

Trenches

The long, steep-sided valleys on the ocean floor are called trenches.

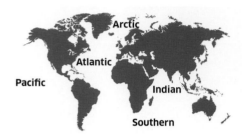

Arctic
Atlantic
Pacific
Indian
Southern

Five Oceans
Geographers divide the planet's water into five oceans: Pacific, Atlantic, Indian, Arctic, and Southern.

Aleutian Trench
About 2050 miles long and more than 24,934 feet deep, the Aleutian Trench is the world's largest.

Liquid Planet

Nearly 71 percent of the planet's surface is covered with water.

Pacific Ocean
Area: 69.5 million sq mi
Average depth: 14,000 ft

Atlanic Ocean
Area: 41 million sq mi
Average depth: 9000 ft

Indian Ocean
Area: 29 million sq mi
Average depth: 12,760 ft

Arctic Ocean
Area: 7.8 million sq mi
Average depth: 3406 ft

Southern Ocean
Area: 5.4 million sq mi
Average depth: 3953 ft

Pacific Ocean

The Deepest Descent

The Bathyscaphe Trieste holds the record for the deepest descent. In 1960, it went down to the Mariana Trench, 35,797 feet below sea level.

East Pacific Rise
The Galapagos Islands and Easter Island lie along this long ocean ridge.

Mid-Atlantic Ridge
This ridge crosses the Atlantic Ocean from north to south. Some of its mountains have emerged as volcanic islands, including the Azores and Iceland.

Ocean Life

Most of the planet's life is found in the oceans and seas. The waters are home to life forms ranging from the microscopic plankton to the largest animals of all, whales.

CURRENTS
The ocean currents are large masses of cold or hot water moving through the oceans.

Blue whale
The largest animal on the planet, the blue whale (above), weighs between 100 and 120 tons.

Mariana Trench
Located in the Western Pacific, the Mariana Trench reaches 36,070 feet in depth. It is the deepest trench in the world.

Arctic Ocean

Atlantic Ocean

Indian Ocean

Pacific Ocean

Types of Seas

 Inland
These seas are surrounded by land, such as the Caspian Sea.

 Coastal
Coastal seas are found in shallow areas along continents' coast.

 Continental
These seas are between land but have a channel to the ocean.

THE ARCTIC

The Arctic is the region north of the Arctic Circle. This region includes the northern parts of Asia, North America, and Europe, together with most of the world's largest island, Greenland. These land areas enclose the world's smallest ocean, the Arctic Ocean. Near its ice-covered center is the North Pole.

Icebergs
Icebergs break away from valley **glaciers** and from Greenland's huge **ice sheet**. Some drift south into the Atlantic Ocean.

The Inuit

The Inuit live in the Arctic region of North America. In 1999, a new Canadian province named Nunavut was established for them.

A Permanently Cold Region

The Arctic is a bitterly cold region and the Arctic Ocean is largely covered with thick ice throughout the year. Temperatures on the central **ice cap** can drop below -85 °F, but ocean currents keep the southwestern coast relatively mild.

Greenland

With the exception of Antarctica, Greenland is the world's least-populated land. As well as the Inuit of Greenland and northern Canada, other Arctic peoples are the Sami found in northern Scandinavia, and the Samoyeds, Tungus, and Yakuts of northern Asia.

18,176 ft
The depth of the Arctic Ocean at its deepest.

EXPEDITION
The first expedition to claim to have reached the North Pole was led by Commander Robert Peary in 1909, but many experts now doubt that he actually got there.

ALASKA (USA)

CHURCHI SEA

Ambarchik

Kolyma

Yukon

Bering Strait

Barrow   ● Pt. Barrow

EAST SIBERIAN SEA

Indigirka

RUSSIA

Mackenzie

BEAUFORT SEA

C.BATHURST

New Siberian Islands

Lena

Banks Islands

CANADA

Victoria Islands

McClure Strait

ARCTIC OCEAN

LAPTEV SEA

● Nordvik

Queen Elizabeth Islands

NORTH MAGNETIC POLE

Severnaya Zemlya

NORTH POLE

Ellesmere Island

Dikson
●

Yenisey

Foxe Basin

Franz Josef Land

LINCOLN SEA

Novaya Zemlya

KARA SEA

Ob

Baffin Island

BAFFIN BAY

Svalbard (Norway)

Pechora

Davis Strait

GREENLAND (DENMARK)

BARENTS SEA

● Nuuk

GREENLAND SEA

North Cape

● Murmansk

Denmark Strait

NORWEGIAN SEA

Archangel
●

ICELAND

● Reykjavik

ANIMALS OF THE ARCTIC

HARP SEAL PUPS

Prey of Hunters

When they are young, harp seals have soft, white fur. The numbers of seals have dropped because the pups are hunted for this fur.

NORTH AMERICAN CARIBOU

Grazing in the Tundra

Caribou are North American deer. They spend the summer grazing on mosses, grasses, and lichens in the Arctic tundra.

Tundra

The mainland areas in the Arctic Circle are covered with a treeless wilderness called the tundra. The most common animals are caribou and reindeer, but bears, foxes, hares, lemmings, and voles are also found here.

Drying White Fish

Although many Arctic people live in settlements today, traditionally they caught different types of fish and hunted seals for food. Fish that was not eaten immediately was hung up to dry and eaten later.

Icebound Ships

The Arctic ice makes shipping conditions difficult. Over the years, ships, including cruise liners and **expeditions**, have all become stuck in the thick ice.

Animal Adaptation

There are several animals found in the Arctic region, including walruses, polar bears, arctic foxes, and birds such as snowy owls. Plants and animals that live in the Arctic have **adaptations** to help them survive and raise young in the extreme cold and windy conditions. For example, some plants found in the tundra have furry or waxlike coatings to protect them against the cold and wind.

Walrus

A thick layer of special fat, called blubber, keeps walruses warm.

Polar bear

Paw pads with rough surfaces stop polar bears from slipping on the ice.

Arctic fox

An extremely thick, long fur coat keeps the Arctic fox warm.

Snowy owl

The snowy owl has feathers on its legs and feet to provide warmth.

CLIMATE

The Earth's climate is a constantly changing system. It is driven by the energy of the Sun. There are five subsystems to our climate: the atmosphere, the biosphere, the hydrosphere, the cryosphere, and the lithosphere. The interactions between these subsystems create different climate zones where the temperature, wind, and rain are all similar.

Rain
Water vapor in the atmosphere condenses to form clouds. When the clouds become heavy enough, the water falls as rain or snow.

Atmosphere

Different types of weather are produced here, including rain, wind, water evaporation, and humidity.

Biosphere

All living organisms—animals and plants—and their habitats are found here. They give energy to the atmosphere.

EVAPORATION

Heat evaporates water from the oceans. It moves into the atmosphere as water vapor.

HEAT

Winds
Winds are caused by the movement of warm and cool air in the atmosphere.

OCEAN CURRENTS

Hydrosphere

This is made up of all the bodies of liquid water on the planet: oceans, seas, rivers, and lakes.

59 °F

The average temperature at the Earth's surface.

SOLAR RAYS

The Sun
The Sun provides energy and drives the changes in each subsystem.

Lithosphere

The lithosphere is the outer layer of the Earth, formed of the continents and the ocean floor. Continuous changes to its surface affect the climate.

Cryosphere

The cryosphere is the parts of the planet that are covered in ice or where the rock or soil is below 32 °F. It reflects almost all of the Sun's rays back into the atmosphere.

HEAT

HUMAN ACTIVITY

VOLCANOES
The particles that volcanoes put into the atmosphere block out sunlight and lower temperatures.

Under the volcano
Here, there is molten rock at temperatures of more than 2012 °F.

Return to the sea
Water seeps into the lithosphere and drains through it into the oceans, or the hydrosphere.

FLORA AND FAUNA

The Earth is divided into different biomes. A biome is an area with a particular climate in which the plants and animals that live there are adapted to the conditions. Different biomes include grassland, tundra, and desert. Factors such as the quality of the soil, altitude, and human activity can affect how each species lives within each biome.

Polar bears
When ice forms over the ocean, polar bears move onto the ice to hunt.

Climate

The Earth's biomes are divided according to the climate in which they are found. Climatic conditions such as wind, temperature, and rainfall determine which organisms live in each biome. Some plants and animals have developed specifically to survive in a certain biome. However, some animals are forced to **migrate** to different biomes with better living conditions.

Distribution
Plants and animals need water to survive. Fewer species are found in habitats where there is less water. These are the world's deserts.

POLAR ZONE

Tundra

SUBPOLAR ZONE

Taiga

HUMANS
Human activity, such as deforestation, has affected many species-rich regions.

TEMPERATE ZONE

Desert · Steppe · Grassland · Forest

TROPICAL ZONE

Desert · Savanna · Forest

Animal Adaptation

Animals have adapted to live in certain biomes. These adaptations ensure their survival. However, when human activity causes changes to their natural habitats, animals find that they have smaller and smaller regions in which to live.

Deserts
Many of the animals that live in deserts, such as the spiny lizard (above), can survive for days on very little food or water.

Polar Regions
Very few species are found in the icy polar regions. Polar bears (above) have a special thick coat to protect them from the cold.

Marine **Biodiversity**
There is a wide variety of species in the world's oceans and seas. Large numbers of species are found in the world's warm tropical waters

Tropical Forests
The tropical forests are home to many different species. This tree frog feeds on crickets, flies, and moths.

Biomes of the World
This map shows the different biomes found on land and in the water.

- Mountains
- Desert
- Grassland
- Taiga
- Temperate forests
- Tropical rain forests
- Polar
- Coral reefs

ANTARCTICA

The Antarctic lies south of the Antarctic Circle. It includes most of the world's fifth-largest continent, Antarctica, in the middle of which is the South Pole. Only the tip of the Antarctic Peninsula, jutting out toward South America, lies outside the Antarctic Circle. The waters around Antarctica are called the Southern Ocean or Antarctic Ocean.

INTERNATIONAL PARK?
Many people would like to make Antarctica a protected area, keeping it safe from development.

Antarctic Circle

Ice covers about 98 percent of Antarctica. The average thickness of the ice is 7218 feet, but in places it is 15,748 feet thick. The region is so cold that there are few plants and animals that can survive the icy temperatures. However, the region is home to penguins. These flightless birds feed mainly on the fish they find in the waters around the continent.

Exploring the Antarctic

Early explorers in Antarctica faced great hardship. An expedition first reached the South Pole in 1911. It was led by the Norwegian Roald Amundsen. A British expedition led by Robert Falcon Scott reached the South Pole five weeks later, but Scott and all his team died on the way back.

S. Orkney Is.
C. Norvegia
Queen Maud Land
S. Shetland Is.
Antarctic Peninsula
WEDDELL SEA
Coats Land
Enderby Land
Palmer Archipelago
Mac Robertson Land
CAPE DARNLEY
Alexander Is.
Berkner Is.
RONNE ICE SHELF
PR. CHARLES MTNS.
Charcot Is.
Palmer Land
PENSACOLA MTNS.
AMERICAN HIGHLAND
BELLINGHAUSEN SEA
Vinson Massif 16,050
SOUTH POLE
GREATER ANTARCTICA
Queen Mary Land
Ellsworth Land
LESSER ANTARCTICA
TRANSANTARCTIC MTNS.
Thurston Is.
Knox Coast
AMUNDSEN SEA
Mt. Kirkpatric 14,855
Siple Is.
Mary Byrd Land
ROSS ICE SHELF
Victoria Land
Wilkes Land
Roosevelt Is.
Mt. Erebus 12,448
ROSS SEA
George V Land
C. Adare
SOUTH MAGNETIC POLE

-128.6 °F
The coldest temperature ever recorded was at the Russian Vostok Station.

Roald Amundsen
In 1911, Amundsen was the first man to reach the South Pole. In 1926, he took part in an expedition that flew over the North Pole. He disappeared in June 1928 while on a rescue mission.

Whopping whale
Blue whales, the largest living animals, feed on krill found in the seas around Antarctica.

Trawling Near Antarctica

The cold waters around Antarctica are rich in marine life, including krill (tiny, shrimplike creatures), squid, seals, fish, and whales. An abundance of fish means the area has excellent trawling conditions.

Tents in the Snow

Scientists exploring Antarctica use specially-designed tents called "Scott's Polar Tents," which are very durable and keep in the heat.

Penguin Parade Adélie penguins, the most common penguins in Antarctica, build nests of pebbles on the coast.

Wandering albatross Found around the Southern Ocean, these birds feed mainly on squid, fish, and krill. They have the widest wingspan of any living bird at 12 feet.

RESEARCH **AND EXPLORATION**

Ice Cave Around the coast of Antarctica, the sea hollows out spectacular caves in the ice.

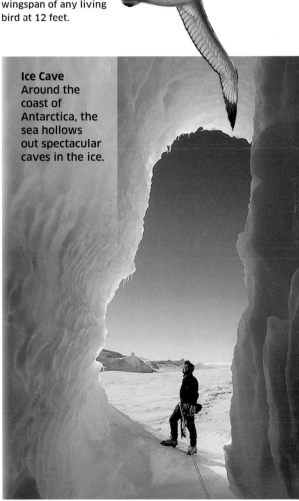

OZONE LAYER **HOLES**

Blocking Harmful Rays

The **ozone layer** in the Earth's upper atmosphere blocks most of the Sun's ultraviolet rays. Pollution has created holes in the ozone layer over Antarctica. Research is being done to discover how this affects the region.

SCIENTISTS **IN ANTARCTICA**

Vital Supplies

There are several research centers in Antarctica. Some have scientists working there all year round, while others are used just in the summer months. Every day, supplies for these scientists are flown or shipped in to Antarctica.

Weather Balloons

Balloons sent up into the atmosphere are used to study weather conditions. The balloons sent up in Antarctica are important because conditions there affect the world's weather.

POPULATION

In 2011, the number of people in the world (the world's population) exceeded 7 billion. However, these people are not spread across the planet evenly. Some areas, such as parts of China, India, and Europe, are densely populated, while other regions, such as Australia and Greenland, have far fewer people living in them.

HUNGER
According to the United Nations, 925 million people in the world do not have enough to eat.

THE 20 MOST-POPULOUS COUNTRIES

1. China 1,343,239,923
2. India 1,205,073,612
3. United States of America 313,847,465
4. Indonesia 248,216,193
5. Brazil 205,716,890
6. Pakistan 190,291,129
7. Nigeria 170,123,740
8. Bangladesh 161,083,804
9. Russia 138,082,178
10. Japan 127,368,088
11. Mexico 114,975,406
12. Philippines 103,775,002
13. Ethiopia 93,815,992
14. Vietnam 91,519,289
15. Egypt 83,688,164
16. Germany 81,305,856
17. Turkey 79,749,461
18. Iran 78,868,711
19. Dem. Republic of Congo 73,599,190
20. Thailand 67,091,089

Population Density

A country's population density is the average number of people living on each square mile of land.

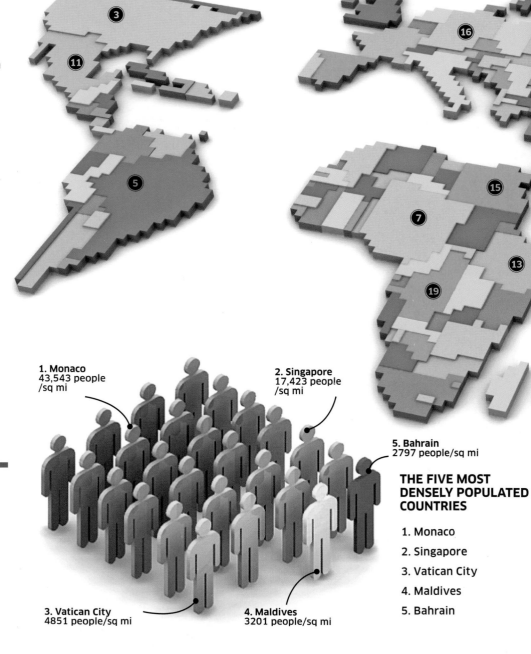

1. Monaco
43,543 people /sq mi

2. Singapore
17,423 people /sq mi

5. Bahrain
2797 people/sq mi

3. Vatican City
4851 people/sq mi

4. Maldives
3201 people/sq mi

THE FIVE MOST DENSELY POPULATED COUNTRIES

1. Monaco
2. Singapore
3. Vatican City
4. Maldives
5. Bahrain

CASE STUDIES
CITY AND COUNTRY

Migration

Migration is the word used for the movement of people from one place to another, both within the same country or from one country to another. People may move in search of work or to leave a war-torn area.

Urbanization

People often migrate from the countryside to live in cities or towns. This is called **urbanization**. Trinidad and Tobago in the Caribbean has a very low level of urbanization. Just 13 percent of people live in cities or towns.

40%
The predicted increase in world population by 2050, according to the United Nations.

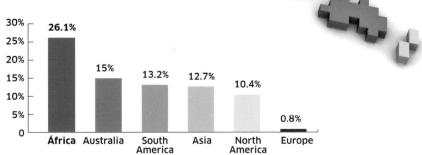

THE THREE MAIN RELIGIONS IN THE WORLD

1. Christianity
2.1 billion followers

2. Islam
1.5 billion followers

3. Hinduism
900 million followers

POPULATION GROWTH 2000–2010

The world's population is growing fastest in less economically developed areas. Many rich parts of the world are already very densely populated.

Region	Growth
África	26.1%
Australia	15%
South America	13.2%
Asia	12.7%
North America	10.4%
Europe	0.8%

THE MODERN WORLD

In recent centuries, human activity has been changing the planet. Large areas of forest have been cut down to make way for farms, while pollution from industry is harming the atmosphere. This is having a serious effect on the environment, and in coming years, we will need to find new ways to live that are less harmful to the planet we depend on.

CARBON
The level of **carbon dioxide** in the atmosphere has increased by 40 percent in the last 150 years.

❶

NEOLITHIC
Humans first started to farm about 10,000 years ago. The farmers built towns to live in and for the first time, people settled in one place rather than moving around as nomads.

❸

INDUSTRIAL AGE
The Industrial Age saw more people living in cities and more manufacturing. The manufacturing caused an increase in pollution.

Distanced from Nature

More people than ever before live in cities, human-made environments that are far from nature. As the population grows, new cities are being built. It is important that cities are planned to make them energy-efficient, meaning that people use less energy to heat their homes and travel to work.

❷

MIDDLE AGES
During the Middle Ages, the walled cities of Europe were very crowded and people lived in poor conditions.

7 billion

The world's population in 2011. A thousand years ago, there were only 300 million people, the population of the United States today.

400 million

The estimated number of dogs in the world.

22,000

The number of polar bears in the world.

❹

21ST CENTURY
Humans begin to find ways to cut down on pollution and to live in less destructive ways.

Overpopulation

The increased number of people in the world is putting a huge strain on the environment. New forms of development that do not destroy the environment are needed. This is called sustainable development.

Threats
Overpopulation is the root of many problems, including hunger, climate change, pollution, and the destruction of wildlife.

CLIMATE CHANGE

In recent years, the average temperature of the Earth has been slowly rising. This increase in average temperature is called global warming. The main cause of global warming is human activity. While the change in temperature both on land and in the sea has been gradual, global warming is changing the world's climate, which is causing serious problems in some parts of the world.

CORAL REEFS
Many coral reefs are dying because of the increase in sea temperature.

THE EFFECTS OF GLOBAL WARMING

The global temperature has increased by a few tenths of a degree in the last few decades. Although this seems like a small change, life on the Earth is delicately balanced, and a small change in temperature can have a serious effect. Global warming has become a major threat to the welfare of all living beings.

50%
The reduction in population of Adélie penguins because of ice loss in Antarctica in the last 30 years.

Thawing at the poles
The rise in temperature is causing large amounts of ice at the polar caps to melt. This leads to an increase in sea level.

Floods
Climate change is causing large floods. In recent years, Bangladesh has seen some of the worst floods in its history.

Islands Under the Water

The small Pacific islands of Tuvalu and Kiribati and the Maldives in the Indian Ocean are very low-lying, which makes them vulnerable to rising sea levels. If the oceans rise just several feet, this will leave the islands completely underwater.

Disappearing glaciers
As a result of global warming, many glaciers in mountainous regions are shrinking.

Desertification
Climate change is causing drought in central Asia. This leads to poor harvests and a shortage of food.

Greenhouse Effect

Greenhouses are specially built to trap heat so that plants can be grown. Similarly, the greenhouse effect is a natural process where the gases in the Earth's atmosphere trap some of the Sun's energy. Without the greenhouse effect, the planet would be too cold to live on.

Carbon dioxide and methane are both greenhouse gases. Carbon dioxide is given off when coal, gas, and oil are burned. Methane is given off by cattle. Increases in the level of both of these gases in the atmosphere means that the average temperature of the Earth is increasing.

Reflected radiation
Part of the Sun's energy is reflected into space.

Sun's rays

Trapped radiation
Some of the Sun's energy is trapped in the atmosphere by greenhouse gases.

Greenhouse gases

Surface of the Earth

NORTH AMERICA INTRODUCTION

The landscape of North America is very beautiful, with a varied range of features. These include the majestic Rocky Mountains in the west and the Appalachians in the east, as well as the dry deserts of California and Arizona. The south and center of the continent are the most vulnerable to natural disasters, such as hurricanes, which cause a lot of damage.

BADLANDS NATIONAL PARK, USA
FOSSILS FOUND IN THESE CLAY FORMATIONS HAVE GIVEN SCIENTISTS A BETTER UNDERSTANDING OF EVOLUTION.

NORTH AMERICA
PHYSICAL MAP

ASIA

ARCTIC OCEAN

Greenwich Meridian

Bering Sea

St Lawrence Is.

Cape Prince of Wales

Bering Strait

Nordostrundingen

Greenland Sea

Nunivak Is.

Point Barrow

Cape Morris Jesup

Yukon

Aleutian Islands

Alaska Pen.

ALASKA RANGE

▲ Mt. McKinley 20,322

▲ Mt. Chamberlin 9019

Beaufort Sea

Queen Elizabeth Islands

Ellesmere Is.

Iceland

Kodiak Is.

Gulf of Alaska

Amundsen Gulf

Banks Is.

Parry Islands

Melville Is.

Devon Is.

GREENLAND

Denmark Strait

MacKenzie

Victoria Is.

Prince of Wales Is.

Baffin Bay

Alexander Arch.

Great Bear Lake

Boothia Peninsula

Baffin Is.

Davis Strait

Arctic Circle

Yukon

COAST RANGE

Great Slave Lake

Melville Peninsula

Queen Charlotte Is.

Southampton Is.

Labrador Sea

Cape Farewell

Vancouver Is.

Fraser

L. Athabasca

Canadian Shield

Hudson Bay

Ungava Peninsula

Hudson Strait

NORTH PACIFIC OCEAN

C. Mendocino

Columbia

Athabasca

ROCKY MOUNTAINS

Nelson

James Bay

Labrador Peninsula

▲ Mt. Rainier 14,409

Missouri

L. Manitoba

L. Winnipeg

Severn

Eastmain

Churchill

COAST RANGE

▲ Mt. Shasta 14,163

Yellowstone

Albany

Newfoundland

Gt. Salt Lake

L. Superior

St Lawrence

Gulf of St Lawrence

Cape Race

▲ Mt. Whitney 14,495

Death Valley

Grand Canyon

Colorado

Californian Pen.

Missouri

L. Michigan

L. Huron

L. Ontario

Niagara Falls

Cape Breton Is.

Kansas

Missouri

L. Erie

Cape Sable

Guadalupe Is.

Gulf of California

Pecos

Arkansas

Ohio

Long Island

APPALACHIAN MTS

Red

Mississippi

▲ Mt. Mitchell 6684

Cape Hatteras

Atlantic Plain

NORTH ATLANTIC OCEAN

SA. MADRE OCCIDENTAL

SA. MADRE ORIENTAL

Rio Grande

Cape San Lucas

Gulf Plain

Bermuda

Cape Canaveral

Florida Peninsula

Tropic of Cancer

Colima Volcano ▲ 13,993

SA. MADRE DEL SUR

Pico de Orizaba 18,406

Gulf of Mexico

Bahamas

Strait of Florida

Bay of Campeche

Yucatán Peninsula

Yucatán Channel

Isthmus of Tehuantepec

Scale

0   1000 miles

Caribbean Sea

KEY

Altitude (in feet)

13,000 or over
6500
1600
650
0
-650 (depression)

Depth (in feet)

0
-650
-6500
-16,500 or over

NORTH AMERICA
POLITICAL MAP

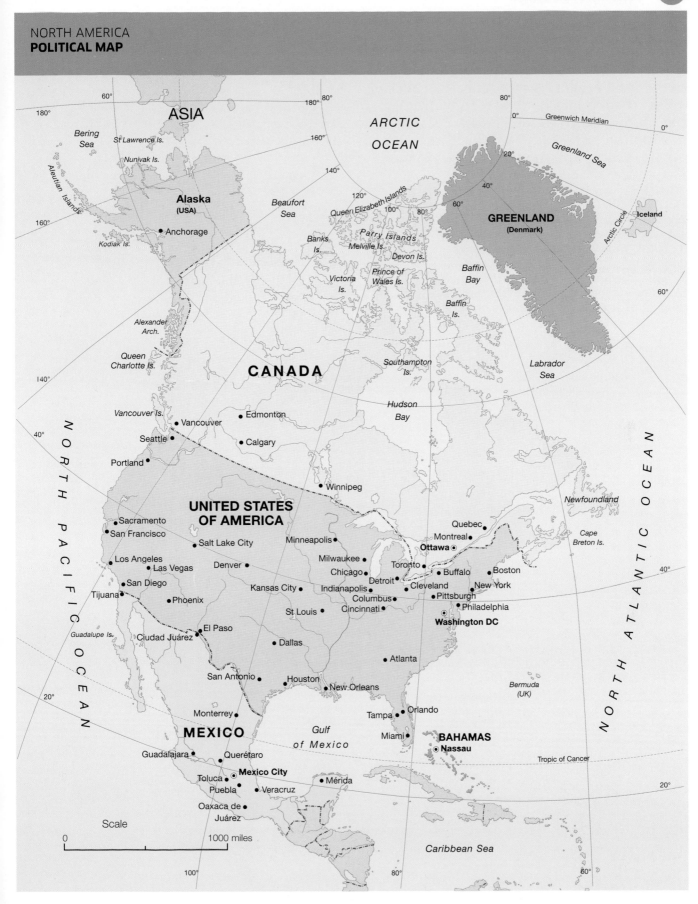

ASIA

ARCTIC OCEAN

Bering Sea
St Lawrence Is.
Nunivak Is.
Aleutian Islands

Greenwich Meridian

Greenland Sea

Alaska
(USA)

Beaufort Sea

Queen Elizabeth Islands

GREENLAND
(Denmark)

Iceland

Anchorage

Kodiak Is.

Banks Is.
Melville Is.
Parry Islands
Devon Is.

Baffin Bay

Alexander Arch.

Victoria Is.
Prince of Wales Is.

Baffin Is.

Queen Charlotte Is.

CANADA

Southampton Is.

Labrador Sea

Vancouver Is.

Hudson Bay

NORTH PACIFIC OCEAN

Vancouver
Edmonton
Seattle
Calgary
Portland

Newfoundland

Winnipeg

UNITED STATES OF AMERICA

Cape Breton Is.

Sacramento
San Francisco
Salt Lake City
Minneapolis
Quebec
Montreal
Ottawa

Los Angeles
Las Vegas
Denver
Milwaukee
Chicago
Toronto
Buffalo
Boston
New York

San Diego
Kansas City
Indianapolis
Detroit
Cleveland
Pittsburgh
Philadelphia

Tijuana
Phoenix
St Louis
Cincinnati
Columbus

Guadalupe Is.

El Paso
Ciudad Juárez
Dallas

Washington DC

San Antonio
Houston
Atlanta

Bermuda (UK)

NORTH ATLANTIC OCEAN

Monterrey
New Orleans

Tampa
Orlando

MEXICO
Gulf of Mexico
Miami

BAHAMAS
Nassau

Guadalajara
Querétaro

Tropic of Cancer

Toluca
Mexico City
Mérida

Puebla
Veracruz

Oaxaca de Juárez

Scale

0   1000 miles

Caribbean Sea

THE ROCKY MOUNTAINS

This mountain chain, also known as the Rockies, runs parallel to the west coast of North America, covering over 3000 miles. The mountains sweep down from northwest Canada to the southwestern United States. They are a popular tourist destination, especially for hiking, camping, fishing, mountain biking, skiing, and snowboarding.

VISITS
More than 3 million visitors go to the Rocky Mountain National Park every year.

Four Regions

The Rockies border the Great Plains to the east and the Rocky Mountain Trench to the west. The mountains are sometimes divided into four sections (right). This includes the Brooks Range, which extends from Canada into Alaska, and is often thought of as an extension of the Rockies.

Labrador Seaway

Hudson Seaway

Western Interior Seaway

Where They Came From

The Rockies are young mountains that formed 75 million years ago. They first appeared when the ocean floor emerged out of the sea in a great arch.

Arctic Province
The Alaska Range is home to North America's highest peak, Mount McKinley, which sits at 20,322 ft.

Northern Province
From British Columbia, the Rockies stretch through Canada and continue into the US states of Washington, Idaho, and Wyoming. This part of the chain is extremely rugged and beautiful, with glaciers in some areas. Mount Robson (12,972 ft) is the highest peak in this region.

Central Province
This region includes Wyoming, and its highest peak is Gannett Peak at 13,802 ft.

Southern Province
This area has the highest **elevation** of the Rockies. Its highest peak is Mount Elbert at 14,432 ft.

Brooks Range

Alaska Range

ALASKA

Mount McKinley

CANADA

Mount Robson

UNITED STATES

Gannett Peak

MOUNT ELBERT

Profile

This profile of the Southern Province Rockies gives an impression of the majestic peaks of the mountains.

■ The Rockies

N
0   mi   621

Comanche Peak 12,703 ft

Electric Peak 10,968 ft

Mount Raddle 12,224 ft

Pikes Peak 14,108 ft

Mount Logan 12,871 ft

Mount Evans 14,265 ft

Longs Peak 14,255 ft

Ypsilon 13,507 ft

Bald Mountain 11,004 ft

Bald Chiquita Mountain 9836 ft

THE APPALACHIANS

The most prominent feature of the landscape in eastern North America is the Appalachian mountain range. These fold mountains formed around 480 million years ago. Mount Mitchell is the highest peak, at 6684 feet.

MINING

Mining in this mountain area is threatening wildlife.

Colorful highlands
Small, colorful shrubs cover the highlands of Appalachia.

American Holly

With its bright red berries, American holly is found in the region.

Cottontail Rabbit

The cottontail rabbit is one of the most common inhabitants of the region.

FACT FILE

Mount Mitchell
Located in North Carolina, east of the Mississippi, Mount Mitchell is the highest point of the Appalachians.

Fauna and Flora
The mountains are home to many different plant and animal species. The most common animals found in the mountains include black bears, deer, and elk, as well as numerous insects and rodents.

Susquehanna River
The Susquehanna River runs through the Appalachians. Its source is in New York State and it crosses through Pennsylvania and Maryland.

MOUNT ST. HELENS

One of the most explosive volcanoes in North America, Mount St. Helens, is found in Washington State. Mount St. Helens was inactive for many years but on May 18, 1980, it erupted. The eruption killed 57 people and there were **avalanches** of **lava** that destroyed 232 square miles of trees. The nearby lake overflowed causing **mudslides** that destroyed houses and highways.

PEAK BEFORE THE EXPLOSION

GLACIER

PATH OF DESTRUCTION
The eruption destroyed 250 houses, 47 bridges, and 186 miles of highway.

OPENING OF THE EXPLOSION

Type of volcano	Stratovolcano
Recent eruptions	1980-1998-2004
Lives lost	57

How Mount St. Helens erupte

Bulge

Old secondary crater

1 Before the eruption, a bulge could be seen on the northern side of the volcano.

9678 ft

After the eruption,
Mount St. Helens
lost its cone shape.

-1316 ft

8363 ft

THE ERUPTION OF MOUNT ST. HELENS

Before and after the Eruption

Mount St. Helens was a striking
feature of the landscape. Before
the eruption, forests and fields
surrounded the volcano. The
eruption left the top of the
volcano as a horseshoe-shaped
pit, with nothing around it.

During the Explosion

The energy released was many
times more powerful than an
atomic bomb. The explosion
lasted more than nine hours.

Volcanic ash burned
trees and destroyed
forests for several miles.

Crater is
blocked

The magma
could not
escape and
pressure built
up on the
northern side

The cone
became
blocked

The crater
explodes

The blockages
caused an
avalanche of
magma and ash

A column of
smoke and
ash rose
12 miles
in height

Profile
before
eruption

Profile
after eruption

2 Pressure built up on
the northern side.

3 Magma and gases erupted
in a huge explosion.

4 The ash eruption appeared
at its most powerful.

THE SEMIDESERT HABITAT

Rainfall is rare in the semidesert, but the small amount of precipitation is what makes the difference between this habitat and a desert. The moisture ensures that cactuses, shrubs, and many other plants can grow. The abundance of these plants at certain times of the year, especially in spring and summer, attracts animal species. In winter, it is very cold and dry, and the wildlife hibernates or seeks shelter.

LOCATION
Semideserts are found in Colorado, Texas, and Montana, in the United States.

Storing Water

Plants with leaves and thick stems, or roots close to the surface, can absorb moisture easily from the rare rainfalls. The cacti leaves will change to thorns, minimizing the moisture they lose and protecting them from hungry animals.

Red-tailed hawk

Gila woodpecker

Elf owl

Pygmy fox

White-tailed squirrel

Tarantula

Ant

Roadrunner
This creature is able to reach a speed of 18 miles per hour to capture its prey of birds, rodents, and reptiles.

Western diamondback rattlesnake

American badger

Saguaro cactus
This cactus's fleshy stem expands like a musical accordion to store water at a volume of 80 percent of its weight. Its stem may reach a height nearly 46 feet, and it can weigh up to 10 tons. Its roots are shallow but can extend up to 98 feet.

The American Semidesert

In winter, the temperature in a semidesert habitat can drop to -22 °F. These harsh conditions cause animals living there to use the vegetation and cactuses as places to shelter. They also provide a source of water.

Coyote

Musk hog

Black-tailed jackrabbit

Desert tortoise

Gila monster

Desert scorpion
This creature has a weapon in its tail that injects venom into its prey.

THE SEMIDESERTS OF NORTH AMERICA

Overview

In the semidesert habitat, only moisture-storing plants, such as cactuses, can survive on the small amount of available moisture. A little more than 8.5 fl oz of rain falls each year.

Plants

Desert plants flourish in this habitat. The ocotillo (below) sheds its leaves once it has absorbed enough moisture to survive, leaving thorns to protect it.

Wildlife

An adult desert tortoise (below) can survive without water for almost a year. Its front legs are specially adapted to dig large, deep burrows, from which it comes out to feed in the morning and evening. It can live for between 50 and 80 years.

OIL EXPLOSION

On April 20, 2010, BP's oil rig Deepwater Horizon exploded in the Gulf of Mexico, 43.5 miles off the coast of New Orleans, and sank two days later. Until the well was sealed in September, thousands of gallons of oil spilled into the ocean each day, having a devastating effect on the environment.

Oil Spill
US officials were quick to establish barriers in order to prevent the spill reaching the coast.

DISPERSANTS OF OIL

How They Work
Chemical dispersants are used to help clean up oil spills. They quickly break the oil down into natural substances.

The dispersant, which contains cleaning chemicals, is applied.

The chemicals get into the oil.

The chemicals reduce the surface tension of the oil.

Oil droplets start to emerge from the layer.

A shiny coat is left once the oil has been broken down.

TEAMWORK
CLEANING THE COAST

The Battle
The success of cleaning up an oil spill depends largely on good organization and teamwork. Sometimes, the oil can be contained using sandbags (right).

Cleaners
To remove oil from coastal rocks, high-pressure washers can be used (right).

Ecological Disaster
The Deepwater Horizon extracted oil from the seabed.

OIL SPILL
NATURAL DISASTER

Fisheries Closed

In Louisiana, oysters and shrimp had to be thrown away because they were exposed to oil (below).

Special Volunteers

Volunteers helped to clean the feathers of pelicans found off the coast of Louisiana.

Environmental Awareness

Environmentalists around the world protested (below) to express their anger over the Gulf of Mexico spill.

Long-Term Poison

The oil spill has harmed deep-water species, such as sea turtles (below), which migrate to the Mexican coast.

CLIMATE

The North American climate can be extreme and very varied—from the icy temperatures of Alaska, to the dry heat of the deserts of Mexico and the southwestern United States. There are also frequent hurricanes and tornadoes.

Hurricane Katrina
Severe floods followed the New Orleans hurricane in 2005.

HURRICANE KATRINA

In the Gulf of Mexico

Starting in the Gulf of Mexico in August 2005, Hurricane Katrina was one of the most powerful **tropical storms** to hit the USA.

Flooding in New Orleans

The strong winds caused by Katrina flooded New Orleans and submerged much of the city (below).

TORNADOES
TEXAS

Swirling Air

Tornadoes are common in the state of Texas. They appear as a column of hot air destroying everything in their path.

THUNDER AND LIGHTNING
GULF OF MEXICO

Moisture and Heat

The Gulf of Mexico causes an excess of heat and moisture in its atmosphere. When hot air collides with cold air, thunderstorms form.

WEATHER ALERT
UNITED STATES

Traffic Chaos

When there is an extreme weather alert, people are told to leave their homes and to travel to a place of safety. This causes traffic problems.

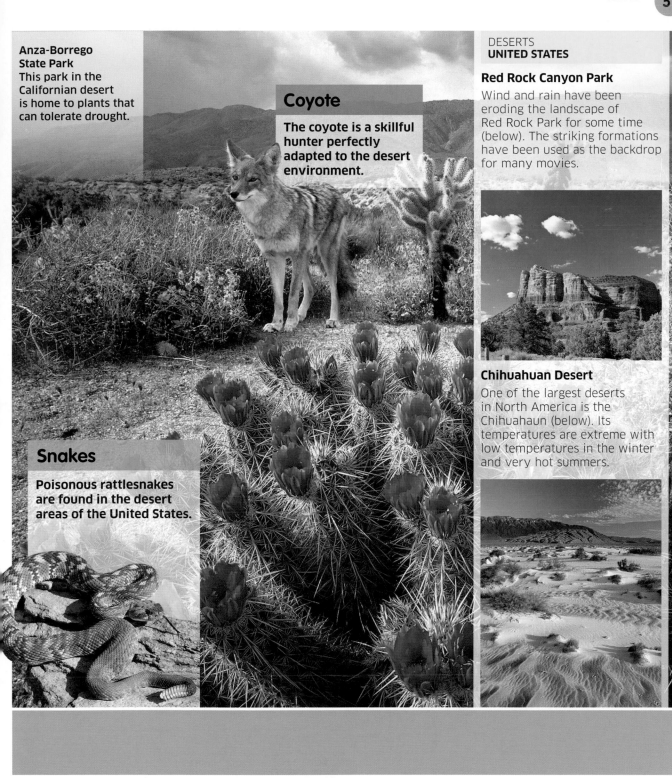

Anza-Borrego State Park
This park in the Californian desert is home to plants that can tolerate drought.

Coyote

The coyote is a skillful hunter perfectly adapted to the desert environment.

Snakes

Poisonous rattlesnakes are found in the desert areas of the United States.

DESERTS
UNITED STATES

Red Rock Canyon Park
Wind and rain have been eroding the landscape of Red Rock Park for some time (below). The striking formations have been used as the backdrop for many movies.

Chihuahuan Desert
One of the largest deserts in North America is the Chihuahaun (below). Its temperatures are extreme with low temperatures in the winter and very hot summers.

Cozumel, Mexico
The island of Cozumel is located 11 miles off the coast of Yucatan. Ocean currents in the Gulf of Mexico cause mild temperatures of about 79 °F, making it a popular tourist destination. It is home to several unique animal species, including the dwarf raccoon.

POPULATION AND ECONOMY

According to the Census Bureau of the United States, the total population in 2012 was 313,136,227, and its population growth is among the highest in **industrialized** countries. Canada and the United States are highly industrialized countries and are considered global powers.

Capitol Hill
This is one of the most iconic buildings in Washington, DC.

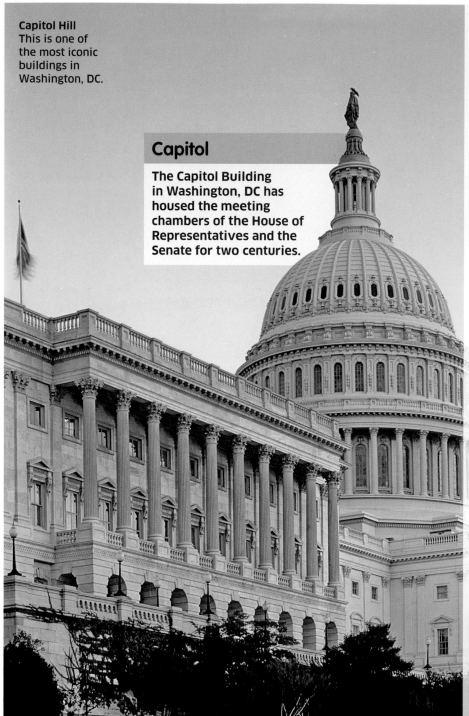

Capitol

The Capitol Building in Washington, DC has housed the meeting chambers of the House of Representatives and the Senate for two centuries.

UNITED STATES
HUMAN GEOGRAPHY

Miami, Florida
Miami (below) is one of the most densely populated cities in the United States, along with New York City.

Cape Canaveral
Cape Canaveral is the main center for US space activities. It is located on the Atlantic coast of Florida.

Silicon Valley, California
High-tech industries have flourished in Silicon Valley, California. The area includes the Santa Clara Valley and the southern half of San Francisco Peninsula.

Palace of Fine Arts
Located in the
historic center
of Mexico City.

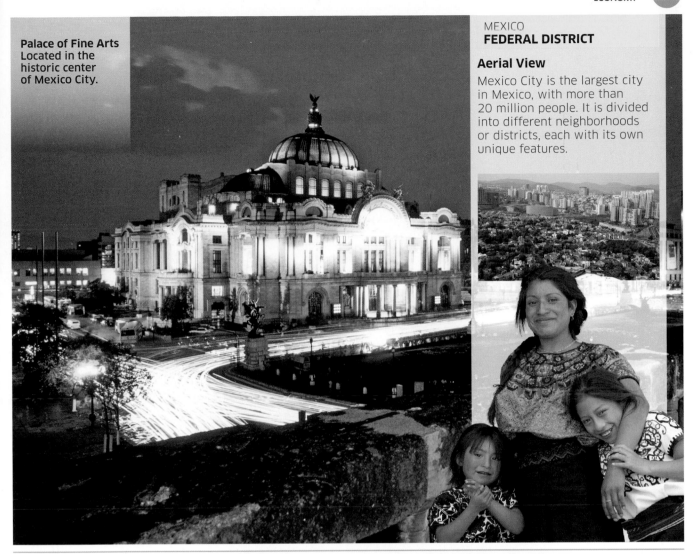

FEDERAL DISTRICT

Aerial View

Mexico City is the largest city
in Mexico, with more than
20 million people. It is divided
into different neighborhoods
or districts, each with its own
unique features.

ECONOMY
CANADA

Industry

Canada is one of the world's most
economically developed countries.
Computer industries, automotives,
electronics, aeronautics, and
chemicals are very important
to the economy. Forests of spruce,
pine, and cedar allow the large-
scale manufacturing of paper
pulp and newsprint.

Nathan Phillips Square
This plaza is at the
heart of downtown
Toronto, Canada.

MEXICO CITY

Although it is crowded and has a high level of pollution, Mexico City is steeped in history. The historic center is built on the ruins of the Aztec capital, and in the elegant district of the Reformation, colonial architecture sits alongside modern buildings.

Country	Mexico
Area	573 sq mi
Population	8,840,000 (city proper)
Density	15,416 people per sq mi

EMBLEM OF THE CITY

The Angel of Independence

The Angel of Independence was built to honor those who fought against Spanish rule. It was erected in 1910 and was designed by Antonio Rivas Mercado. The monument is located in the Paseo de la Reforma avenue, which connects the center of the city with Chapultepec.

The Winged Victory
The bronze statue (right and below) shows an angel in flight with open arms. In her right hand she holds a wreath.

Burritos
Typical Mexican food includes burritos. Filled with meat and vegetables, these tortilla wraps (below) are served with spicy sauces.

The Cathedral

This is the largest cathedral in Latin America and dominates the main square of Mexico City. The church and its chapels are ornately decorated.

The Zócalo
A view of the main square.

Women's Collective

Buses used exclusively by women and children (left) run along the main city streets. There are also different subway lines, buses, and trains.

Frida Kahlo Museum

The artist Frida Kahlo lived and died in the neighborhood of Coyoacan. Today, this house (left) is a museum that exhibits many of her personal items, such as her bed and dresses.

National Palace

The National Palace is an important government building in Mexico. The staircase walls and two courtyard walls are decorated with colorful murals by the Mexican painter Diego Rivera.

THE CITY SQUARE

The Zócalo is one of the largest squares in the world. Flags fly in its center and on public buildings, restaurants, and hotels.

PARKS AND PROMENADES
CHAPULTEPEC AND XOCHIMILCO

Restful Places in a Busy City

Xochimilco (below) is the only place in Mexico City that still houses the floating gardens (or chinampas), built by the Aztecs.

Chapultepec Park is an enormous green area (bottom) in the middle of this bustling city.

Population

Mexico's constitution recognizes 62 different groups of peoples in the country who have strong links with this region throughout history. This ensures that their culture and language are protected.

THE STATUE OF LIBERTY

One of the world's most famous monuments stands on Liberty Island, south of Manhattan, in New York City. The monument is called "Liberty Enlightening the World" and was a gift from France to the United States in 1886.

TECHNICAL DESCRIPTION

Opened:
October 28, 1886

Location:
Liberty Island,
New York

Construction:
The figure is made from copper plates. Due to the size and weight of the stone base, it rests on four gigantic steel supports.

IN DETAIL

Support
The statue's strength is created by an internal tower. A skeleton around this tower keeps the outer layer of copper in place.

Plaque
Inside the statue is a plaque with the poem "The New Colossus" by Emma Lazarus.

Base
The base is square and rests on a star-shaped plinth.

Museums
There are two museums at the foot of the statue.

Head
To reach the head, visitors must climb 354 steps. It is 16 feet from the chin to the skull.

The Sculptor

The statue is the work of the French sculptor Frédéric Auguste Bartholdi. An ancient statue, the Colossus of Rhodes, inspired him.

Torch
The torch was originally made from copper, but in 1916, it was changed to 600 pieces of yellow glass to enhance its brightness. The flame is covered with gold leaf.

Manhattan
The statue gives tourists some of the best views of Manhattan Island. With a population of just over 8.1 million, Manhattan is considered one of the largest urban areas in the world.

Crown
There are seven points in the statue's crown. They symbolize the seven seas and the seven continents of the world.

Elevator

An elevator goes as far as the 10th floor. The 12 further floors must be reached by foot.

Tablet
There is a tablet in the left hand that bears the date of US Independence.

328 ft
The height of the statue from the base to the torch.

Vision
The statue was the first thing **immigrants** saw when they arrived by boat in the United States.

Statue
Close-up view of the famous monument.

CENTRAL AMERICA AND THE CARIBBEAN INTRODUCTION

Central America and the Caribbean separate North and South America. The region has areas of volcanic activity as well as places of great natural beauty. The warm tropical climate produces lush vegetation, such as rain forests. The warm, clear waters of the Atlantic Ocean and the Caribbean Sea are home to beautiful coral reefs.

INCREDIBLE HABITAT
THE BELIZE RAIN FOREST IS HOME TO THOUSANDS OF SPECIES OF ANIMALS AND PLANTS.

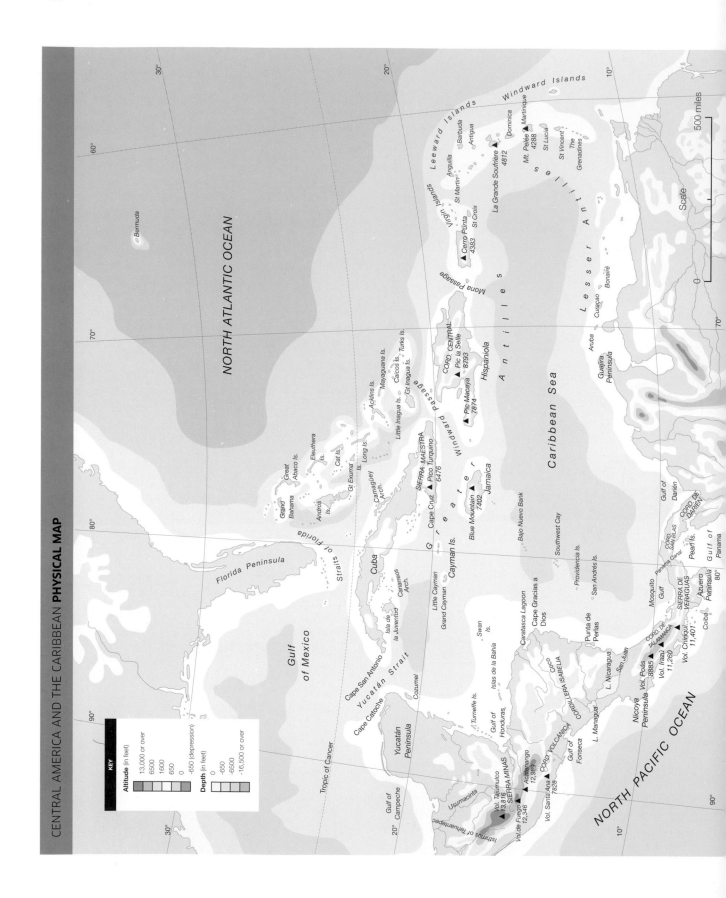

CENTRAL AMERICA AND THE CARIBBEAN **PHYSICAL MAP**

KEY

Altitude (in feet)
13,000 or over
6500
1600
650
0
-650 (depression)

Depth (in feet)
0
-650
-6500
-16,500 or over

NORTH ATLANTIC OCEAN

Bermuda

Florida Peninsula

Straits of Florida

Gulf of Mexico

Tropic of Cancer

Cape San Antonio

Yucatán Strait

Cape Catoche

Cozumel

Yucatán Peninsula

Gulf of Campeche

Isthmus of Tehuantepec

Usumacinta

Vol. Tajumulco 13,816
SIERRA MINAS
Acatenango 12,989
CORD. VOLCANICA
Vol. Santa Ana 7828
Vol. de Fuego 12,346

Gulf of Honduras

Turneffe Is.
Islas de la Bahía

Gulf of Fonseca

L. Managua
L. Nicaragua
San Juan

CORDILLERA ISABELIA
COCO

Nicoya Peninsula

Vol. Poás 8885
Vol. Irazú 11,260
CORD. DE TALAMANCA
Vol. Chiriquí 11,401
SIERRA DE VERAGUAS
Coiba
Azuero Peninsula
CORD. DE SAN BLAS
Panama Canal
Gulf of Panama

CORD. DE DARIÉN
Gulf of Darién
Pearl Is.

NORTH PACIFIC OCEAN

Cuba
Isla de la Juventud
Canarreos Arch.

Little Cayman
Grand Cayman
Cayman Is.

Swan Is.
Caratasca Lagoon
Cape Gracias a Dios
Punta de Perlas

Mosquito Gulf

Providencia Is.
San Andrés Is.

Southwest Cay
Bajo Nuevo Bank

Grand Bahama
Great Abaco Is.
Eleuthera Is.
Andros Is.
Cat Is.
Gt Exuma Is.
Long Is.
Camagüey Arch.
Acklins Is.
Mayaguana Is.
Caicos Is.
Turks Is.
Little Inagua Is.
Gt Inagua Is.

SIERRA MAESTRA
Pico Turquino 6476
Cape Cruz

Jamaica
Blue Mountain 7402

G r e a t e r   A n t i l l e s

Windward Passage

Pic Macaya 7874
Pic la Selle 8793
CORD. CENTRAL
Hispaniola

Mona Passage

Cerro Punta 4383

Virgin Islands
St Martin
Anguilla

Leeward Islands
St Croix
Barbuda
Antigua

La Grande Soufrière 4812
Dominica
Mt. Pelée 4288
Martinique
St Lucia
St Vincent
The Grenadines

Windward Islands

L e s s e r   A n t i l l e s

Aruba
Curaçao
Bonaire
Guajira Peninsula

Caribbean Sea

Scale
500 miles
0

30°
20°
10°

60°
70°
80°
90°

70°

20°
30°

10°
90°

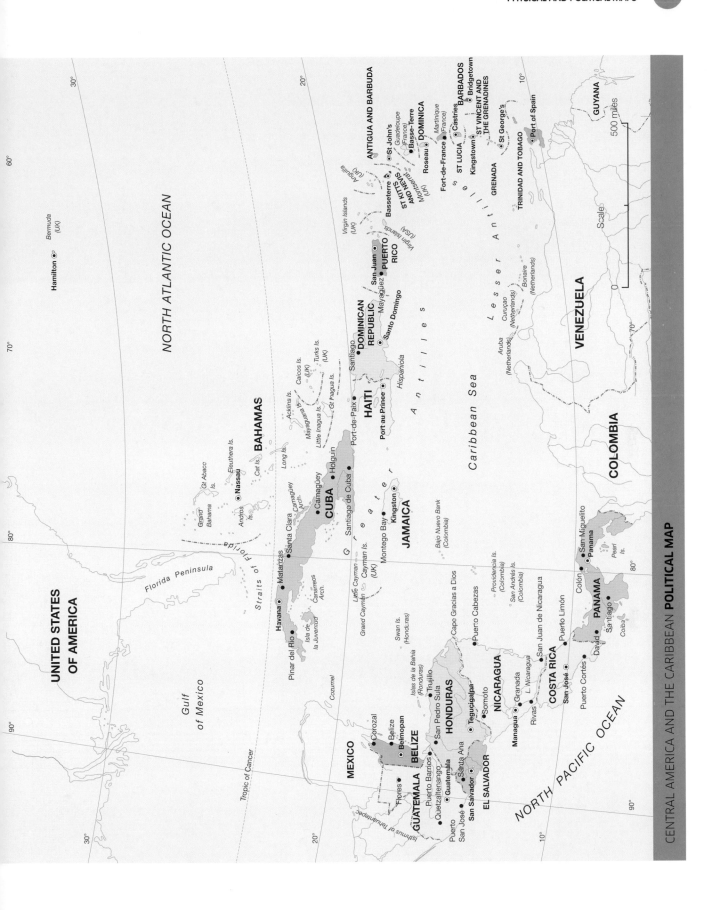

CENTRAL AMERICA AND THE CARIBBEAN **POLITICAL MAP**

FLORA AND FAUNA

Mountains, sea-washed shores, and tropical rain forests are found throughout Central America and the Caribbean. The region's plants and animals are very varied. Alligators, iguanas, and coral reefs are all found here.

Kinkajou

The kinkajou, also known as the honey bear, lives in Central America. It is a **nocturnal** mammal that lives in trees and feeds on fruits.

Jaguar

The jaguar (left) is the largest carnivore in the Americas and one of the largest worldwide. This cat is in danger of **extinction**.

Macaw

The red-and-green macaw (left) nests in hollow trees in the region's forests. It feeds on seeds and fruit.

Quetzal

With its brightly colored feathers and long tail, the quetzal is the national bird of Guatemala.

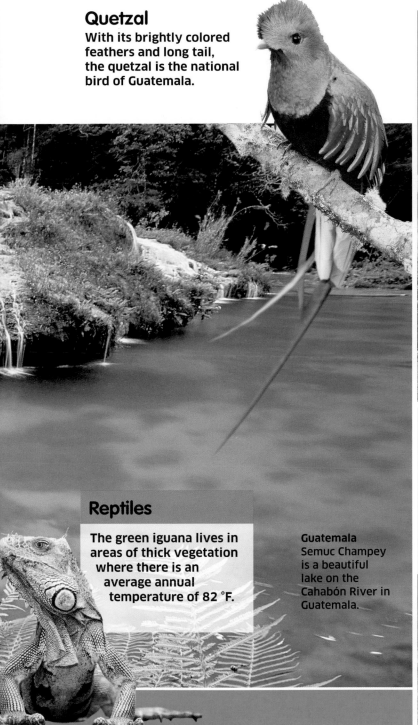

Reptiles

The green iguana lives in areas of thick vegetation where there is an average annual temperature of 82 °F.

Guatemala
Semuc Champey is a beautiful lake on the Cahabón River in Guatemala.

Silvertip Shark

The silvertip shark is found in the Pacific Ocean. It reaches a maximum length of 10 feet. It is a danger to humans.

NATURE RESERVE
TIKAL NATIONAL PARK

Forest Ruins

The Tikal National Park is found in the Petén region of Guatemala. The park is home to pumas, jaguars, birds such as toucans, and parrots, and many species of monkey. Tikal was once one of the biggest cities of the Mayan civilization. The ruins of the city lie in the park.

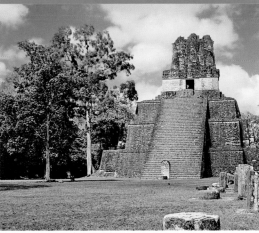

COLORFUL
MARINE LIFE

Coral Reefs in Belize

Beautiful coral reefs lie just off the shore of Belize. The reefs are about 186 miles long. They are the second largest in the world, after the Great Barrier Reef in Australia. These reefs are home to many different species of fish.

POPULATION AND ECONOMY

Much of the population of Central America and the Caribbean descended from Africans, Europeans, and Asians. The economies of most of the countries are based on tourism and agriculture. Bananas, cotton, sugar cane, and tobacco are some of the most widely-grown crops.

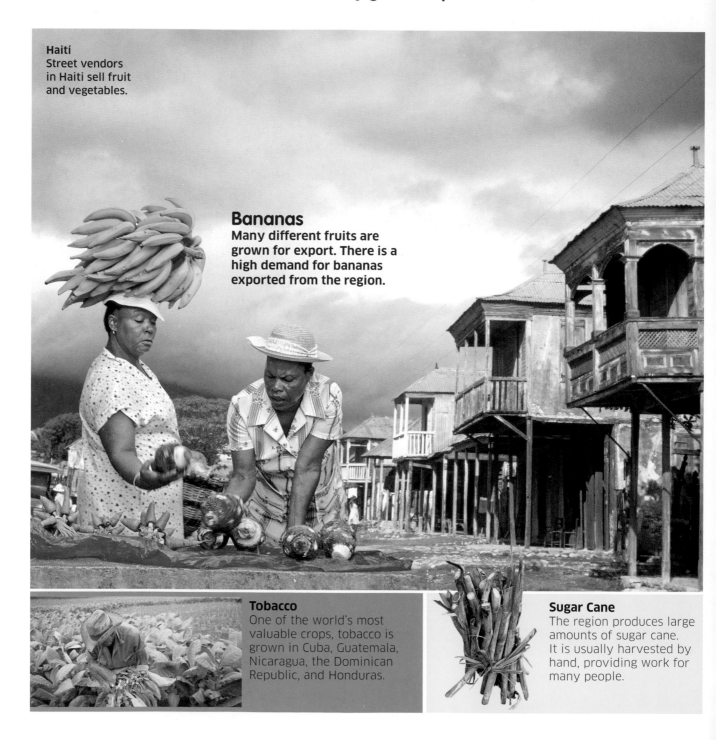

Haiti
Street vendors in Haiti sell fruit and vegetables.

Bananas
Many different fruits are grown for export. There is a high demand for bananas exported from the region.

Tobacco
One of the world's most valuable crops, tobacco is grown in Cuba, Guatemala, Nicaragua, the Dominican Republic, and Honduras.

Sugar Cane
The region produces large amounts of sugar cane. It is usually harvested by hand, providing work for many people.

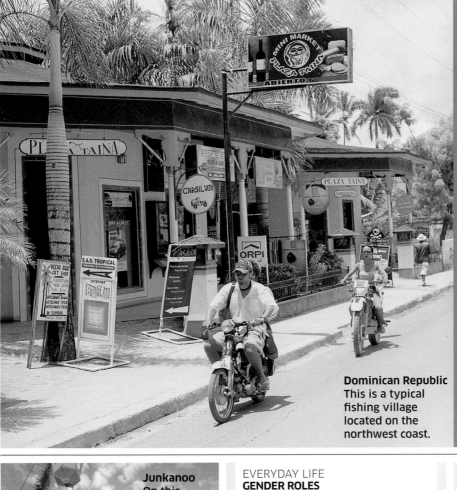

Dominican Republic
This is a typical fishing village located on the northwest coast.

MAIN ETHNIC GROUPS

African Heritage

African influences can be seen in many aspects of daily life in the region. For example, there is music that has developed from African traditions, such as the mambo. Many of the people also hold spiritual beliefs that are based on African religions.

Junkanoo
On this holiday in the Bahamas, the biggest parade takes place in Nassau.

EVERYDAY LIFE
GENDER ROLES

Role of Women

In this region, women often have to work harder than men. Recent studies confirm that women spend more time in unpaid activities than men.

LOSS OF CROPS
HEAVY RAINS

Honduras

In 2010, heavy rains fell across Honduras. This caused landslides that destroyed many homes and ruined many of the crops.

THE PANAMA CANAL

A work of engineering brilliance, the Panama Canal allows ships to move between the Atlantic and Pacific oceans without going around South America. The first ship passed through the canal in 1914. In 2007, building began on an extension of the canal.

LAKE

CHAMBER

CHAMBER

Ocean to Ocean

It is 50 miles from one ocean to the other, traveling through the Panama Canal.

There and Back

There are two parallel channels, one for raising the water level and the other for lowering it.

CHAMBER

The Lake

At the center of the canal is a lake, which is 85 feet above sea level. Its water fills the locks.

CHAMBER

Building Works

Currently, 14,000 ships cross the canal each year. Once the building works are completed, 18,000 ships will pass through the canal.

How the Locks Work

1 The water in the first lock chamber must be at sea level. To reach sea level, it releases 100 million gallons of fresh water in just eight minutes.

2 When its water is at sea level, the ship enters the first chamber. The valves and dampers are then closed, and the water is returned to the lock to raise the water level.

3 Water flows out of the second chamber to lower its level to the same as the first chamber. The ship passes into the second chamber, and the process is repeated for the third chamber.

8–10 hours
The average time taken to travel through the canal by boat.

THE NEW CANAL
WORK BEGAN IN 2007

Large Ships
For decades, most of the world's **cargo** was carried on ships that were specifically built to travel through the canal. However, many of today's ships are now too large to pass through the canal.

Giant Locks
Two new locks (positioned next to the current canal) will make it possible for these larger ships to travel through the canal. The new canal will also have a system of pools to save fresh water.

Pools are used to stop fresh water from the lake entering the ocean.

CHAMBER

CHAMBER

POOLS

OCEAN

LAKE GATUN
One of the largest artificial lakes in the world, Lake Gatun is 163 square miles.

NEW CANAL

CURRENT CANAL

Ship fitting new canal

Depth: 49 ft

12,000 containers

1201 ft

161 ft

Ship fitting old canal

Depth: 39 ft

4500 containers

965 ft

105 ft

SOUTH AMERICA INTRODUCTION

This large continent extends from the northern hemisphere down close to the Antarctic Circle. It has a huge range of climates, from tropical rain forest and hot desert, to the dry cold of Patagonia in southern Argentina. Most of the continent forms part of an area called Latin America, which is made up of the former colonies of Spain and Portugal. For this reason, Spanish and Portuguese are the most widely spoken languages. There are also a large number of other languages and cultures on the continent. In the Amazon Rain Forest, there are still a few small groups of people who have never contacted the outside world.

THICK CLOUDS
THE ANDES MOUNTAINS RUN ALONG THE WEST OF THE CONTINENT, PARALLEL TO THE PACIFIC COAST.

SOUTH AMERICA
PHYSICAL MAP

NORTH
ATLANTIC
OCEAN

Caribbean Sea

Guajira
Peninsula
Panama
Canal
L.
Maracaibo

Lesser Antilles

Margarita Is.
Trinidad
Orinoco Delta

G. of Venezuela

NORTH

PACIFIC

OCEAN

CORD. DE MÉRIDA

Orinoco
Orinoco
Plains
PACARAIMA MTS.

Angel Falls

GUIANA SHIELD

Cape Grande

Amazon
Estuary

Marajó
Is.

Amazon

Nevado
del Tolima
17,110

CORD. OCCIDENTAL

CORD. ORIENTAL

Pico da Neblina ▲
9990

Negro

Branco

C. de Sao Roque

Fernando
de Noronha

Equator
Galápagos
Is.

0°

Punta Galera
Cotopaxi ▲
19,347
Chimborazo ▲
20,561

A
N
D
E
S

Japurá

Tocantins

Amazon

0°

Gulf of Guayaquil
Punta Negra

Sechura
Desert

Juruá

Ucayali

Amazon Basin

Madeira

Tapajós

Xingu

Tocantins

Paranaíba

BORBOREMA
PLATEAU

Paulo Afonso Falls

Nevado Huascarán ▲
22,132

CORD. ORIENTAL

CORDILLERA OCCIDENTAL

Paresis Tableland
Guaporé

Araguaia

Sao Francisco

B. de Todos os Santos

Mamoré

PLATEAU OF
MATO GROSSO

BRAZILIAN
HIGHLANDS

SOUTH

L. Titicaca
Nevado Sajama ▲
21,463
L. Poopó

Río de la
Plata Basin

Pico da Bandeira ▲
9482

Gulf of
Arica

Pilcomayo

Paraguay

Paraná

20°

PACIFIC

20°

Tropic of Capricorn

Llullaillaco ▲
22,057

Salado

Bermejo

Gran Chaco

Iguazu Falls

Cape Frío

SOUTH

OCEAN

Mt Pissis ▲
22,286

Paraná

Uruguay

CUCHILLA
GRANDE

Patos Lagoon

ATLANTIC

Mt. Aconcagua ▲
22,841
Tupungato ▲
21,490

Pampas

Mirim Lagoon

Río de la Plata

Juan
Fernández

Colorado

Cape San Antonio

KEY

Altitude (in feet)

13,000 or over
6500
1600
650
0
-650 (depression)

Lanín ▲
12,388

Negro

Bahía Blanca

OCEAN

L. Nahuel
Huapi

Valdés Pen.

40°
20°

Depth (in feet)

0
-650
-6500
-16,500 or over

Chiloé Is.

Gulf of
San Jorge

A
N
D
E
S

Taitao
Pen.

L. Buenos Aires

▲ Mt. Fitz Roy
11,020

Bahía
Grande

Argentine Sea

Falkland Is.

South Georgia

L. Argentino

0   Scale   1000 miles

Tierra del Fuego

I. de los Estados

Cape Horn

Drake   Passage

80°   60°   40°   20°

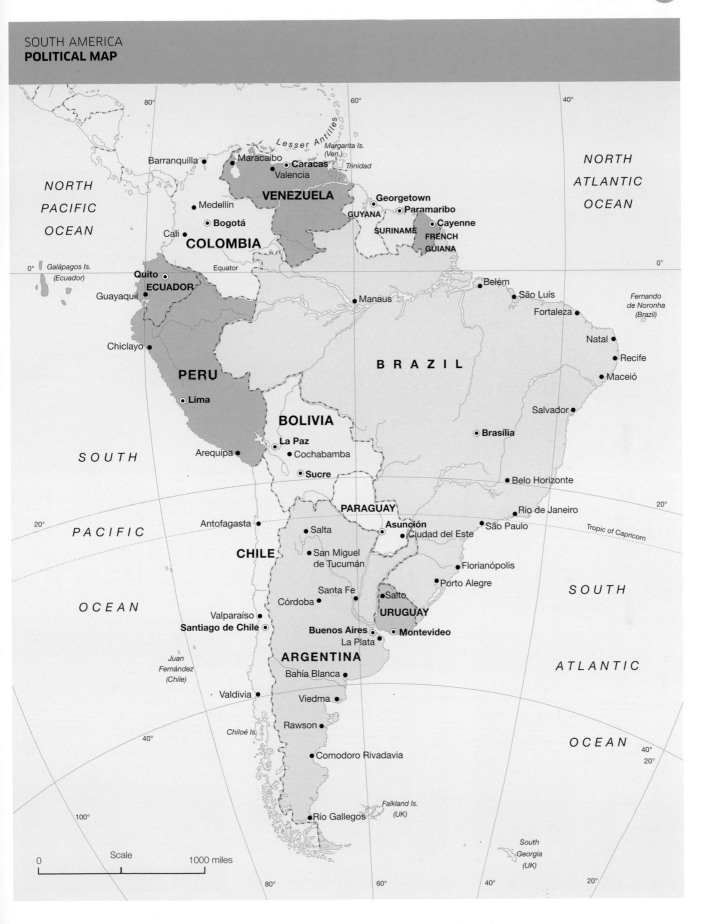

SOUTH AMERICA
POLITICAL MAP

80°   60°   40°

NORTH
ATLANTIC
OCEAN

Barranquilla   Maracaibo
                 Caracas   *Margarita Is.*
                 Valencia   *(Ven.)*
                                 Trinidad

NORTH
PACIFIC
OCEAN

Medellín   **VENEZUELA**   **Georgetown**
                                   Paramaribo
Bogotá   **GUYANA**   **Cayenne**
Cali   **SURINAME**   **FRENCH**
COLOMBIA   **GUIANA**

0°   *Galápagos Is.*   Equator   0°
        (Ecuador)

Quito   Belém
ECUADOR   São Luís   *Fernando*
Guayaquil   Manaus   *de Noronha*
                                                  Fortaleza   *(Brazil)*

Chiclayo   **B R A Z I L** Natal

                                                  Recife

PERU   Maceió

Lima   Salvador

                 BOLIVIA   **Brasília**

SOUTH   **La Paz**
Arequipa   Cochabamba
                 Sucre   Belo Horizonte

                                                  Rio de Janeiro   20°
20°   **PARAGUAY**
PACIFIC   Antofagasta   **Asunción**   São Paulo   *Tropic of Capricorn*
                 Salta   Ciudad del Este
CHILE   San Miguel
                 de Tucumán   Florianópolis   *SOUTH*
OCEAN   Santa Fe   Porto Alegre
                 Córdoba   Salto
Valparaíso   **URUGUAY**   *ATLANTIC*
Santiago de Chile   **Buenos Aires**   **Montevideo**
                 La Plata
Juan   **ARGENTINA**
Fernández   Bahía Blanca
(Chile)
Valdivia   Viedma   *OCEAN*
                                                                         40°
40°   Rawson   20°

100°   Comodoro Rivadavia

                                  Falkland Is.
                 Río Gallegos   *(UK)*

0   Scale   *South*
                                  Georgia
        1000 miles   *(UK)*

80°   60°   40°   20°

FLORA AND FAUNA

South America boasts a wide range of landscapes and environments. In the tropical forests, there is a rich diversity of animal and plant life, while very different organisms survive in the cold south, or high in the Andes Mountains.

Water lilies
In the Wetlands of
Pantanal, Brazil.

AMAZON
BASIN

Abundance of Life

The largest rain forest in the world lies around the giant Amazon River. More species of animal and plant live here than anywhere else on the planet. The Amazon is the second-longest river in the world, but the largest in terms of volume of water. It contains 20 percent of all the river water in the world.

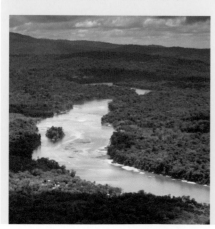

DESERT SCRUB
ANDES – PATAGONIA

Tough Species

This dry environment extends from Colombia in the north to Argentina in the south. It follows the Andes Mountains and includes regions of high **plateau** and the coastal deserts of Chile and Peru. Vegetation is mostly grassland. The animals living here have adapted to survive in tough conditions.

DIVERSITY
THE ANDES MOUNTAINS

High Living

The mountain landscape includes dry areas with sparse vegetation and forested areas, such as the Yungas in Bolivia. Many different species of tree grow in the mountain forests. The condor, the Andean flamingo, and the guanaco (a large mammal similar to a camel) can be found in the Andes.

Buzzard Eagle

This bird of prey has special feathers that stop it from freezing to death when it flies over the Andes.

Guianan Cock-of-the-rock

This beautiful bird lives in high rocky areas. It feeds mainly on fruit.

FINE WOOL

Alpacas grow high-quality wool, which is excellent for knitting warm clothing.

Alpaca

The alpaca is very common on the high plains of Ecuador, Bolivia, Chile, and Peru.

Carnivore

The leopard seal is one of the largest predators in the Southern Ocean.

Snake
The red-tailed boa lives in northern South America.

Piranhas

There are several species of piranha in the Amazon River. These **carnivorous** fish can sometimes come together into large schools to attack their prey. However, they rarely attack humans.

Patagonian Woods

Larch, myrtle, and monkey puzzle (above, from left to right) are three of the trees found in Patagonia. Below are the most common plant species that grow there:

1. Verbena
2. Antarctic beech
3. Larch
4. Myrtle
5. Lenga beech
6. Monkey puzzle
7. Hazel

Iguanas and Crabs

The Barrington Land iguana (left) and the red rock crab (below) both live on the Galápagos Islands, a remote group of islands in the Pacific Ocean that has many unique species. Studying the animals and plants here helped Charles Darwin to formulate his theory of evolution by natural selection.

CRISIS IN THE AMAZON

One-fifth of the Amazon Rain Forest has been cut down by humans since 1970. However, there are encouraging signs that the rate of destruction is slowing down, as the governments of Brazil and other countries take action. Further destruction of the Amazon could damage the whole world's climate.

Amazon Basin

Brazilian Amazon

DEFORESTED AREAS
In these areas all the trees have been cut down.

FIRES
Fires have been used to clear land for agriculture.

URBAN AREAS
Development of urban areas is unplanned and growing.

PROTECTED AREAS
National parks that cannot be cut down.

INDIGENOUS AREAS
These areas have some protection.

WHAT IS AT STAKE?
ISSUES THAT AFFECT US ALL

Oxygen
Plants in the Amazon produce about 20 percent of oxygen on Earth. They act like the "lungs of the planet."

Greenhouse Effect
Trees absorb carbon dioxide from the air, slowing down global warming. Without the rain forest, the planet will get hotter more quickly.

Biodiversity
An estimated 10 percent of all the known species of plant and animal live in the Amazon Basin.

Culture
It is thought that about 200,000 indigenous people live in the area. Their diverse cultures could be lost.

AMAZON BASIN
MANY COUNTRIES

A Huge Area
The Amazon Basin extends across an area of about 2.7 million square miles crossing several countries. Half of the rain forest lies in Brazil. The rest is spread across Peru, Bolivia, Colombia, Venezuela, Guyana, and Suriname.

Aerial view
The Amazon River empties approximately 261,590 cubic yards of water into the ocean every second.

Rate of Loss
By 1991, the Amazon had lost 160,232 square miles of forest. By 2000, that number had risen to 226,642 square miles. The cleared land is used to graze livestock and to grow crops. The rate of loss has been slowing in recent years.

People in Danger
Many small groups of people call the Amazon home, such as the Yanomami (pictured left). These groups are in danger of losing their way of life, and with it, a huge amount of knowledge about the forest and its plants will be lost.

Rubber
Rubber trees are grown along the banks of the Tapajos River in Brazil. The rubber is collected from cuts made in the bark.

POPULATION

Many people across South America are moving from the countryside to the cities. This has caused rapid and disorganized growth as makeshift homes are built on the outskirts of large cities. These poor urban areas are known as favelas, or shantytowns.

Rio de Janeiro
A view of this Brazilian city, home to more than 6 million people.

Carnival

In Brazil, the biggest and most important festival is called Carnival. People take to the streets in ornate costumes to have a huge party.

BRAZIL
PORTO ALEGRE

Skyscrapers and Highways

Porto Alegre is the capital city of the state of Rio Grande do Sul. It has a population of nearly 1.5 million and is a center for industry and business.

Salvador da Bahia

The first capital city of Portugal's New World Empire, Salvador was founded in 1549. It is one of the oldest cities in Brazil. The historic city center has been made a UNESCO World Heritage Site. It has a population of about 3 million people.

VENEZUELA
CARACAS

Booming City

With a population of more than 3.5 million inhabitants, Caracas is the ninth-largest urban area in Latin America. It is a commercial center that sees a lot of investment from Venezuelan companies and also from abroad.

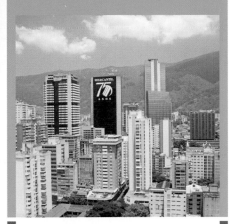

COLOMBIA
BOGOTA

Cultural Center

Colombia's main museums and most important universities are found in its capital city, Bogota. It has a population of more than 6.5 million people. Below is an image of the historic Church of St. Francis in the city.

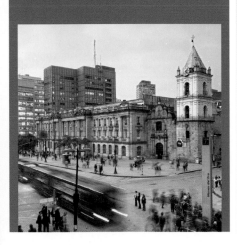

La Boca
A suburb of the city of Buenos Aires, the capital of Argentina.

ARGENTINA
CORDOBA

Second City

The second-largest city in Argentina after Buenos Aires, Cordoba has a population of 1.3 million people. It is known as "the learned one" because the country's best university is found there. Below is the city's cathedral.

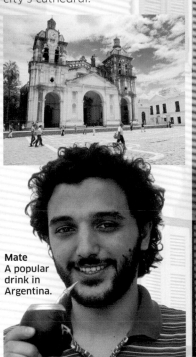

Mate
A popular drink in Argentina.

CHILE
SANTIAGO DE CHILE

High Life Expectancy

With a population of more than 5 million people, Chile's capital city, Santiago, is the largest city in the country. The city contains a rich mix of fine old and striking new architecture. Chile is the country with the longest life expectancy in South America, at around 79 years.

ECONOMIC RESOURCES

South America produces a lot of food for export to other parts of the world. It also has many natural resources and some of the largest oil reserves on the planet. Brazil has the largest economy in South America, followed by Argentina, Colombia, Venezuela, Peru, and Chile.

ARGENTINA
TOURISM

Favorite Destination

The Perito Moreno Glacier is a popular tourist attraction. The drive to the glacier from El Calafate takes in a series of lakes, streams, woods, and snow-capped mountains.

Wonder
The huge glacier is a spectacular natural wonder.

VENEZUELA
OIL

Important Reserve

Oil is the main source of income in Venezuela. Today, a state-owned company manages the country's reserves, which are among the largest in the world. As of January 2011, it had 297 billion barrels left (1 barrel = 42 gallons). In 1960, Venezuela was one of the founding members of OPEC, an association of oil producers around the world. It also has reserves of natural gas, methane, iron, gold, and diamonds. Venezuelan industry concentrates on oil refinery and petrochemicals, which are chemicals made using oil. Its exports are mainly products made from oil or steel. It also has textile, timber, and pharmaceutical industries.

Maracaibo
A center for oil production.

URUGUAY
AGRICULTURE AND TOURISM

Sunflowers

The second-smallest country in South America, Uruguay is known for its fine beaches, such as Punta del Este. Its economy is based around cattle farming and other agriculture. Among the crops grown are soy, wheat, barley, oats, rice, corn, and sunflowers (below).

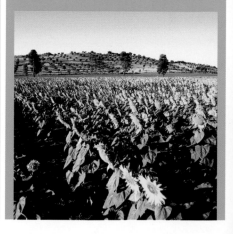

CHILE
MINING

Taking Full Advantage

Mining is the most important industry in Chile, in particular copper mining, which is very profitable. Pictured left is the Chuquicamata mine in the Atacama Desert. Wine-making is another important industry, and Chile exports wine around the world. A typical Chilean vineyard is shown below.

Chuquicamata
This is an open-pit mine.

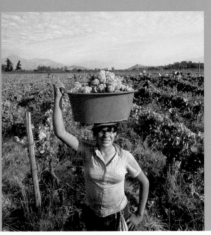

BRAZIL AND COLOMBIA
COFFEE AND MUCH MORE

Powerful Economies

Brazil has traditionally been a large producer of coffee. However, a growing financial sector means that the service sector is now the largest part of the economy, followed by industry. Colombia is still a large producer and exporter of coffee.

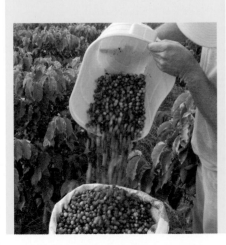

Exploitation
The Amazon has lost much of its forests, cut down to make way for human activity.

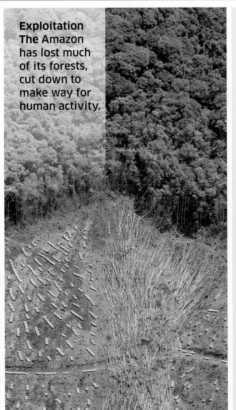

BOLIVIA
ABUNDANT NATURAL GAS

Source of Energy

Bolivia has the second-largest reserves of natural gas in South America. It exports the gas to its neighbors, in particular Brazil and Argentina. It also has smaller oil reserves and many different minerals are mined. The picture below shows some typical gas tankers.

THE NAZCA LINES

The Nazca Lines are drawings on the land in south Peru, some of them more than 984 feet long. They are line drawings of animals, plants, and geometric shapes, which can be seen only from a great height. The lines were drawn on the plain and on the hillsides by the Nazca people, who lived there between 200 BC and AD 500.

PERU
NAZCA

Location
The lines are found in the provinces of Palpa and Nazca on the Pampas de Jumana.

World Heritage Site
In 1994, UNESCO declared the drawings a World Heritage Site.

Entry and exit
The Spider has an entrance and an exit, which allow you to follow the lines without ever crossing from one line to another.

Strange features
The shape and features of the Spider show that it is based on a species from the Amazon Rain forest.

The Spider
One of the best-known figures, the Spider, is made from one continuous line.

Anthony F. Aveni
A scientist from the USA, Aveni linked the lines to water supplies. He believed that they were used in rituals to secure water for crops.

LEGACY OF THE NAZCA

Cultural Works

The Nazca were fine craftspeople. They made good cloths and their pottery was the best in pre-Columbian South America.

Head Trophy
This trophy was found in a tomb.

Two-Headed Snake
A sacred symbol commonly found in the Andes.

Siku
The Siku is a traditional Andean musical instrument.

Cemetery

Nearby, there is a cemetery dating from pre-Columbian times. This mummy was found there.

Map of the Stars

Some researchers, such as Maria Reiche, have suggested that the Spider is a representation of the star formation Orion.

The ground
The surface is covered with a layer of dark reddish stones.

The Spider. Viewed from the air.

BUENOS AIRES

A fascinating city, Buenos Aires is the most densely populated city in Argentina. In the center of the city, there are many historical buildings next to the Plate River. At Puerto Madero nearby, there are stunningly modern developments.

SYMBOLS OF THE CITY

The Teatro Colón

This magnificent concert hall has some of the best **acoustics** in the world. This means that the audience can hear the music clearly.

Avenida 9 de Julio

At 459 feet wide, this is one of the widest streets in the world. The Obelisk, a famous monument, stands at the junction with Corrientes Avenue.

Town Hall

This building has stood for nearly all of the country's 200 years of independence.

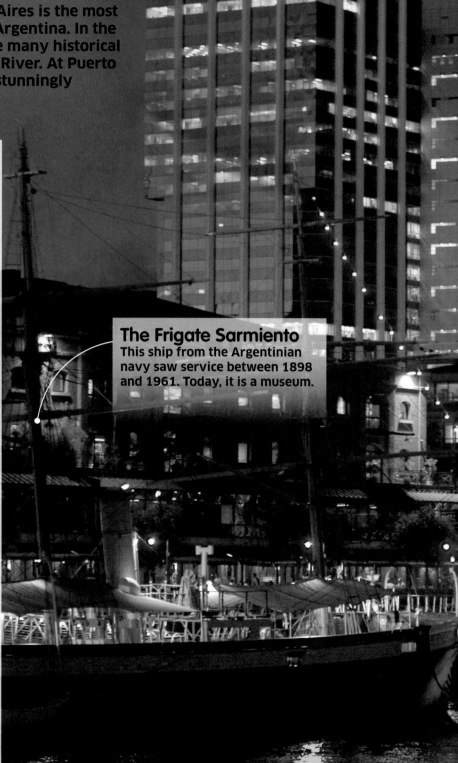

The Frigate Sarmiento

This ship from the Argentinian navy saw service between 1898 and 1961. Today, it is a museum.

Country	Argentina
Area	78 sq mi
Population	2,891,082
Density	37,073 people/sq mi

Night Scene
Puerto Madero has striking new developments, restaurants, and homes.

Puerto Madero
The old port area has seen massive development, with a new residential district and a business center.

NAME
Puerto Madero is named after Eduardo Madero, who drew up the original plans for the port in 1882.

CULTURE IN BUENOS AIRES

Museums
The city has a wide range of museums, including the Proa (top), the Malba (bottom), the Museum of the Fine Arts, and the Museum of Modern Art.

Lezama Park
This park was once a farm owned by the Lezama family. It contains a wide range of different trees, winding paths, a large pergola, waterfalls, monuments, stairways, and an **amphitheater**.

Underground
The city's underground railroad system has six lines. The first station opened in 1913. It was the first underground to be built in South America and is one of the busiest in the world.

CHRIST THE REDEEMER

The majestic statue of Christ the Redeemer stands with arms outstretched over the center of Rio de Janeiro in Brazil. It is built on the rocky summit of Mount Corcovado, 2326 feet above sea level. It is surrounded by the Tijuca Forest, the largest area of urban woodland in the world.

CHRIST THE REDEEMER
FACT FILE

Height:
125 feet

Outer covering:
Greenish-gray soapstone

Weight:
635 tons

Interior:
The structure is made of hollow reinforced concrete

CULTURAL AND RELIGIOUS WORK

Historical Facts

The statue took five years to build and was opened on October 12, 1931. It was a technical challenge because the area is very windy, and it was very difficult to build the outstretched arms and the bent head. The project was run by the engineer Heitor da Silva Costa. The artist Carlos Oswald came up with the final design, while the sculptor Paul Landowski (below) made the head and the hands.

Coating
Soapstone from Minas Gerais was chosen because bad weather and changes in temperature do not damage it.

Church
At the foot of the statue is a small church.

Height
From the base
to the head it is
125 feet, including
the 26-foot plinth.

Head
The head is bent
downward slightly.

2003
The year that
escalators were
installed to carry
people to the base
of the statue.

Symbol
The imposing statue
is one of the largest
religious images in
the world and has
become a symbol
of Brazil.

Interior
Contains beams
and staircases.

Arms
Each arm is
89 feet long.

Mountain Train
The Corcovado Railway
was opened in 1884.
Trains climb through
the lush Tijuca Forest at
a steady 7.4 mi/h. The
trains carried the pieces
of the statue up to the
top of the mountain.

THE AMERICAS GEOGRAPHICAL WONDERS

Mountains, high plateaus, vast plains, deserts, jungles, volcanoes, and glaciers: North, Central, and South America offer a series of spectacular and varied landscapes. There are also large areas of land that are still untouched by humans, many of them now protected as World Heritage Sites.

ALBERTA
CANADA

Banff National Park

Bow Lake in Banff National Park, Alberta, freezes over every winter. Covering an area of 2564 square miles, the park is home to glaciers, woods, and mountains. UNESCO has declared the park a World Heritage Site.

Glacier landscape
Tire tracks run over the surface of a frozen lake near the Canadian Rockies.

CANADA TO NEW MEXICO
UNITED STATES

The Rocky Mountains

This mountain range extends for more than 3000 miles from northern Canada to New Mexico in the south. A young mountain range, it was formed from a series of separate mountain chains that joined together. Between the peaks, the valleys are home to spectacular forests and lakes.

CALIFORNIA
UNITED STATES

San Andreas Fault

The North American and Pacific tectonic plates collide at the San Andreas Fault, which runs parallel to the coast of California and through the city of San Francisco. It is a very unstable area, prone to devastating earthquakes.

CANADA
NORTH AMERICA

Canadian Shield

The Canadian Shield is an ancient chain of eroded mountains that runs alongside Hudson Bay. It forms the shape of a huge horseshoe and has an average height of 984 feet.

CENTRAL AMERICA AND THE CARIBBEAN

Irazu Volcano

With a height of 11,260 feet, Irazu is the highest active volcano in Costa Rica. The summit has five craters. One of the craters is filled with a green lake (left).

Sierra Maestra

Surrounded by lush vegetation, the Sierra Maestra is a mountain chain in southeastern Cuba. Pico Turquino is the highest peak in the Sierra Maestra, reaching 6476 feet above sea level.

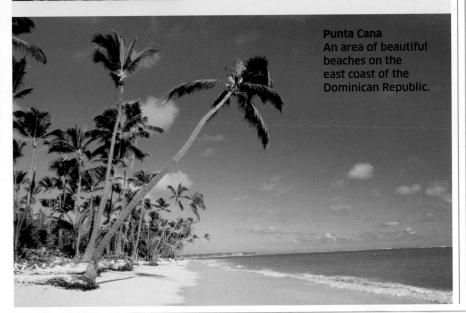

Punta Cana
An area of beautiful beaches on the east coast of the Dominican Republic.

SOUTH AMERICA
AMAZON BASIN

The Great River

The Amazon is the largest river in the world (by volume of water). About 200 smaller rivers flow into it emptying it into the Atlantic Ocean through a huge delta. From the Andes, it flows 4186 miles across South America.

Atacama Desert

The Atacama is one of the driest places on the planet. It extends through the north of Chile between the Copiapo River and the Loa River. Parts of the desert contain rock formations that look like the surface of the Moon.

ARGENTINA
EL CALAFATE

Perito Moreno Glacier

Measuring 18.6 miles long and 3 miles wide, the Perito Moreno Glacier is found in the province of Santa Cruz. Every now and then, there are spectacular crashes of ice as large chunks fall off the front of the glacier.

PEOPLE AND LANGUAGES

Spanish and English are the most widely-spoken languages in the Americas. French and Portuguese are also spoken, as are a wide range of indigenous languages, such as Quechua, Guarani, and Mapuche.

Spanish

Spanish was introduced by the Conquistadors. Since then, the language of each region has changed, developing its own vocabulary and accent.

ORIGINS
The population of the Americas is descended mainly from Amerindians, Africans, and Europeans.

English
The main language of science, trade, and diplomacy.

Culture
Many smaller cultures across the world are in danger of disappearing. Along with them, their languages are lost.

Saving Languages
Anthropologists
believe that it is vital to save languages because they give us different ways of seeing the world.

ORIGINAL LANGUAGES OF THE AMERICAS

Canada and the United States
There are more than 300 native languages, but many are in the process of dying out.

1. Algonquian-Ritwan
2. Caddo
3. Hokan
4. Iroquois
5. Kiowa-Tano
6. Muskogee
7. Others

Mexico and Central America
Quiche and Yucatec are Mayan languages that are still spoken. Many others have disappeared.

1. Macro-Chibcha
2. Maya
3. Mixe-Zoque
4. Oto-Manguean
5. Totonac
6. Uto-Aztecan
7. Others

South America
More than 1000 languages have died out. Some, such as Quechua, are still spoken.

1. Arawak
2. Carib
3. Macro-Chibcha
4. Macro-Ge
5. Pano-Tacanan
6. Quechumaran
7. Others

MAIN NATIVE LANGUAGES
IMPORTANT FACTS

PERU
QUECHUA

Widely Spoken Language
Peru has a great ethnic diversity. Quechua, the language spoken by the Incas, is the language most spoken. It is also spoken in Bolivia, Ecuador, Colombia, Argentina, and Chile.

MEXICO
NAHUATL

A Range of Languages
In Mexico, about 6 million people speak a range of more than 60 native languages. Nahuatl, the Mayan languages, and Zapotec are the most common.

CHILE
MAPUCHE

Influence
The Mapuche, also known as the Araucanians, live in southern Chile and southwest Argentina. Many of their neighbors adopted their language.

CARIBBEAN
CREOLE

African Roots
In Haiti and Dominique, most people speak Creole, which is a language that mixes French vocabulary with the grammar of West African languages.

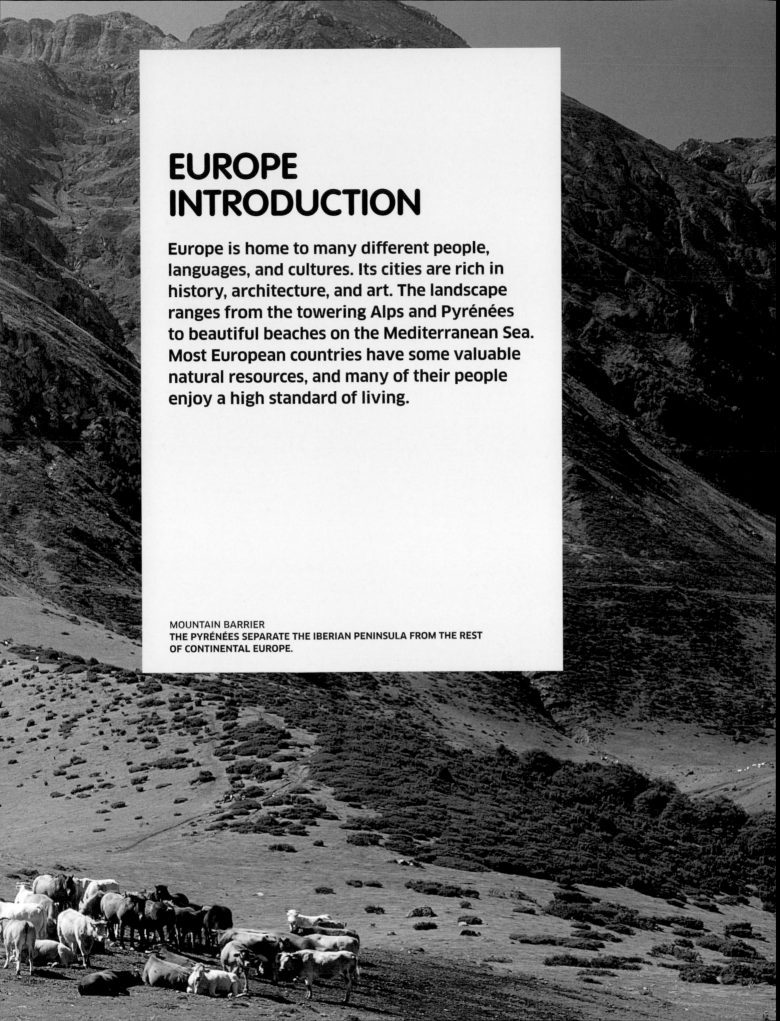

EUROPE INTRODUCTION

Europe is home to many different people, languages, and cultures. Its cities are rich in history, architecture, and art. The landscape ranges from the towering Alps and Pyrénées to beautiful beaches on the Mediterranean Sea. Most European countries have some valuable natural resources, and many of their people enjoy a high standard of living.

MOUNTAIN BARRIER
THE PYRÉNÉES SEPARATE THE IBERIAN PENINSULA FROM THE REST OF CONTINENTAL EUROPE.

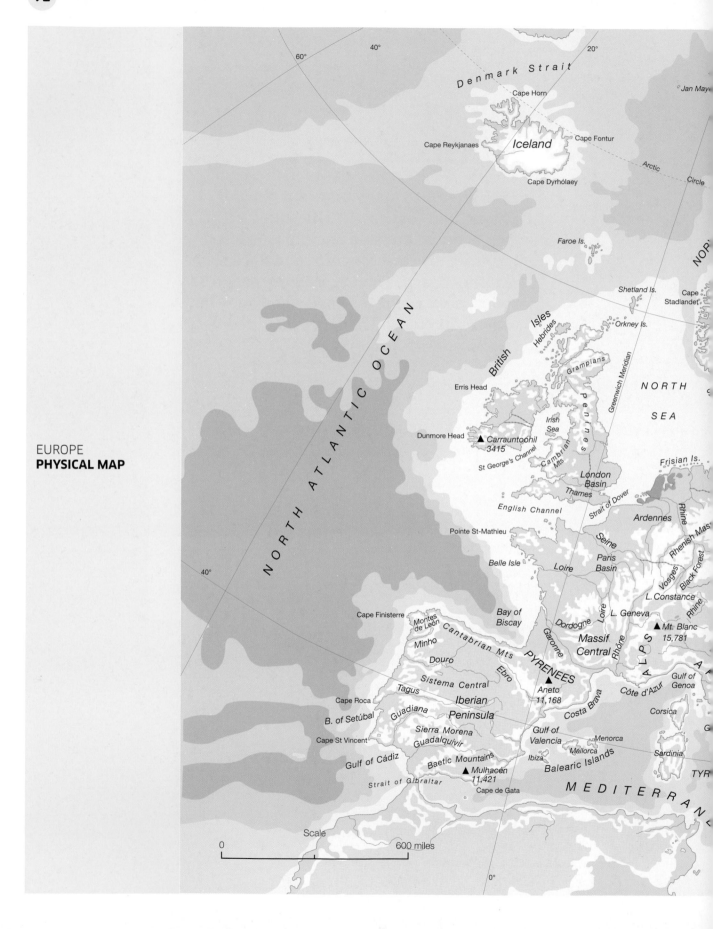

EUROPE
PHYSICAL MAP

Denmark Strait

Cape Horn

Jan May

Cape Reykjanaes

Iceland

Cape Fontur

Arctic

Circle

Cape Dyrhólaey

Faroe Is.

NOR

Shetland Is.

Cape
Stadlandet

British

Isles

Hebrides

Orkney Is.

Grampians

Greenwich Meridian

NORTH
SEA

Erris Head

Penines

Dunmore Head

▲ Carrauntoohil
3415

Irish
Sea

Cambrian
Mts

Frisian Is.

St George's Channel

London
Basin

Thames

Rhine

English Channel

Strait of Dover

Ardennes

Rhenish Mass

Pointe St-Mathieu

Seine

Rhine

Vosges

Black Forest

Belle Isle

Loire

Paris
Basin

L. Constance

L. Geneva

NORTH ATLANTIC OCEAN

Cape Finisterre

Bay of
Biscay

Dordogne

Loire

Rhône

▲ Mt. Blanc
15,781

40°

Montes
de León

Cantabrian Mts

Garonne

PYRENEES

Massif
Central

ALPS

A

Minho

Ebro

Gulf of
Genoa

Douro

Sistema Central

▲
Aneto
11,168

Côte d'Azur

Tagus

Iberian

Costa Brava

Corsica

Cape Roca

Guadiana

Peninsula

B. of Setúbal

Gulf of
Valencia

Menorca

Sierra Morena

Mallorca

Sardinia

Cape St Vincent

Guadalquivir

Ibiza

Gulf of Cádiz

Baetic Mountains

Balearic Islands

TYR

▲ Mulhacén
11,421

Strait of Gibraltar

Cape de Gata

MEDITERRAN

Scale

0   600 miles

0°

20°   40°   60°   80°   60°

O C E A N

BARENTS
SEA

Novaya
Zemlya

Kara Strait

Vaygach
Is.

Northern
Urals

Mageröya Is.
Cape Nordkinn
Söröya Is.
Varanger Fjord
Senja Is.
Finnmark Plateau
...a Is.
L. Inari

Cape
Kanin Nos
Kolguyev Is.
Chesha Bay
Pechora
Narodnaya
1894

URAL
MOUNTAINS

Kola
Peninsula
WHITE SEA
Timan Ridge
Mezen
Pechora

Central Urals

Kebnekaise
6932

Scandinavian Mountains
Lule
Skellefte
Gulf of Bothnia
L. Oulu
L. Vyg
Onega
Northern Dvina

Kama
Reservoir
Mt. Yamantau
5381

Southern Urals

L.
Päijänne
L. Saimaa
L.
Onega
L. Näsijärvi
L.
Ladoga

Kama
Belaja

L. Malaren
Gulf of Finland
L. Peipus
Saaremaa
Valdai
Hills
Rybinsk
Reservoir
Gorky
Reservoir
East
European
Plain
Volga
Msta
...nern
Gotland
Öland

BALTIC SEA

Kuybyshev
Reservoir

Volga

Moksa
Khopyor
Volga Upland
Volga
Saratov
Reservoir
Ural

Western Dvina
Neman
Central Russian Upland
Oka
Desna
Don
Volgograd
Reservoir

ropean Plain
Vistula
Pripyat
Dnieper
Kiev
Reservoir
Seversky Donets
Donets
Ridge
Don

Volga

Caspian Depression

ARAL
SEA

Oder
Vistula
Beskids
Podolian Upland
Dniester
CARPATHIANS
Dnieper
Kremenchug
Reservoir
Kakhovka
Reservoir
SEA OF
AZOV
Kuban
Manych
Kuma

Volga

CASPIAN SEA

40°

Transylvanian
Alps
Moldavian Plateau
Danube
Karkinit
Bay
Crimea
CAUCASUS
MOUNTAINS
Mt. Elbrus
18,510

...ic Alps
Prokletije
Morava
BALKANS
Maritza
Rhodope
Mts.
Balkan
Peninsula
Pindus
Mountains
Thasos
Lemnos
SEA OF
MARMARA
Bosphorus

BLACK SEA

...ATIC SEA
Morava

Mt. Parnassus
8068
Euboea
AEGEAN
SEA
Lesbos

IONIAN
SEA
...na
SEA
...8
Ionian Is.
Peloponnese
Milos
Cyclades
Cape Matapan
SEA OF CRETE
Crete
Rhodes
Karpathos
Cyprus

KEY	
Altitude (in feet)	
	13,000 or over
	6500
	1600
	650
	0
	-650 (depression)
Depth (in feet)	
	0
	-650
	-6500
	-13,000
	-19,500

20°   40°

EUROPE
POLITICAL MAP

20°   40°   60°   80°   60°

Novaya Zemlya

A N

BARENTS SEA

• Vardö
• Pechora

Narvik •
• Inari
• Murmansk

Bodö •
• Rovaniemi

• Gällivare

• Luleå
• Arkhangelsk

A S I A

EDEN
• Storuman
Oulu •
• Belomorsk
• Syktyvkar

• Östersund
• Vaasa
• Kuopio
F I N L A N D
• Petrozavodsk
• Perm

• Borlänge
Tampere •
• Kazan

arlstad
Turku •
Kotka •
R U S S I A
(European area)

tockholm •
• Helsinki
• St Petersburg

• Tallinn
• Samara

ourg
ESTONIA
Tartu •
• Tver

mar •
LATVIA
• Moscow

nö •
• Riga
• Siauliai
• Daugavpils
• Smolensk
• Saratov

LITHUANIA
• Vitebsk
ARAL SEA

Gdynia •
RUSSIA
• Vilnius
• Borysaw

Szczecin •
• Kaliningrad
• Grodno
• Minsk
• Kursk
• Volgograd

POLAND
BELARUS
• Pinsk
• Astrakhan

Walbrzych •
Warsaw •
Lublin •
• Kiev
• Kharkiv
CASPIAN SEA

ECH •
• Kraków
Rivne •
• Zhytomyr

JBLIC
UKRAINE
• Donetsk
• Rostov

SLOVAKIA
• Mukachevo
• Stavropol

a •
• Bratislava
MOLDOVA
• Chisinau
• Odessa
• Sochi
• Makhachkala

• Budapest
40°

ilA
HUNGARY
ROMANIA
• Sebastopol

jana
• Zagreb
• Timisoara

BOSNIA AND
• Belgrade
• Bucharest
BLACK SEA

ERZEGOVINA
Giurgiu •
• Varna

arajevo
SERBIA
BULGARIA

MONTENEGRO
KOSOVO
• Sofia
A S I A

Podgorica •
• Pristina
• Plovdiv

• Skopje
• Istanbul

Tirana •
MACEDONIA
TURKEY

ALBANIA
• Thessaloniki
(European area)

anto
GREECE

eggio •
• Patras
• Athens
Piraeus

use •
• Kalamata

A
• Heraklion
Crete

20°   40°

BALTIC SEA

GEOGRAPHICAL WONDERS

Europe is the second-smallest continent in the world after Oceania. It is mostly very flat, with an average height of just 984 feet. However, the mountain ranges of Europe, such as the Pyrenees, the Alps, and the Caucasus, reach as high as 16,404 feet.

ATLANTIC HEIGHTS
SCANDINAVIA AND ICELAND

High Peaks

The highest peaks in northern Europe are found in Scandinavia. Mount Galdhøpiggen, in Norway, is the highest in the region at 8100 feet.

Alpine Ranges
Typical Alpine landscapes have lakes surrounded by snow-capped peaks.

WESTERN EUROPE
ITALY–FRANCE

Mont Blanc

The most famous peak in Europe is Mont Blanc. Officially, it is 15,781 feet high. However, the layer of snow at the summit can add between 33-49 feet, depending on the time of year. The peak lies on the border between France and Italy.

SPAIN
LA MANCHA

Spain's Central Plains

La Mancha is the largest plain on the Iberian Peninsula. The plain is split in two by the mountains of Toledo. The highest summits are Villuercas, at 5253 feet, and Rocigalgo, at 4747 feet. The area is famed for its traditional windmills.

RUSSIA
GLACIAL LAKES

The Valdai Plateau

The Valdai plateau is located halfway between the Russian cities of St. Petersburg and Moscow. The great plateau is drained by the Volga and Dnieper rivers, among others. Throughout the area, there are many beautiful glacial lakes.

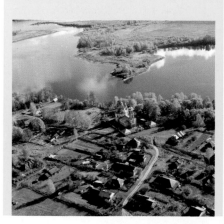

CAUCASUS – RUSSIA
MOUNT ELBRUS

Highest Peak

Mount Elbrus is the highest peak in Europe at 18,510 feet high. The mountain is located on the northern edge of the Caucasus Mountains, near the Russian-Georgian border. Mount Elbrus is a volcano that has been dormant for more than 2000 years. Its summit is covered by a permanent layer of ice and more than 20 glaciers. The mountain is very popular among skiers and snowboarders.

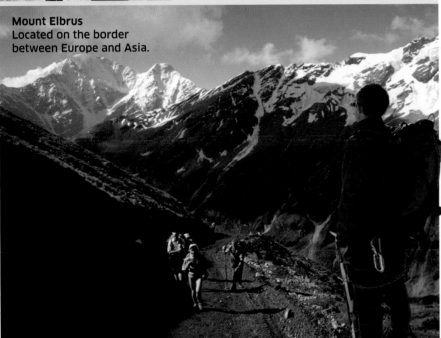

Mount Elbrus
Located on the border between Europe and Asia.

RUSSIA
RIVER SYSTEMS

Floodplains

The gently flowing rivers in western Russia deposit mud and rock as they pass by, to create areas called alluvial floodplains. The soil in the floodplains is rich in nutrients and is used to grow all kinds of crops, including cereals, potatoes, and beets.

THE ALPS
IN PROFILE

Mountain chains, such as the Alps, are formed by folds and breaks in the Earth's crust. **Erosion** wears away the mountains, and rivers carve valleys that separate one mountain from another. High plateaux, such as the Massif Central in France, are often found next to the rocky peaks.

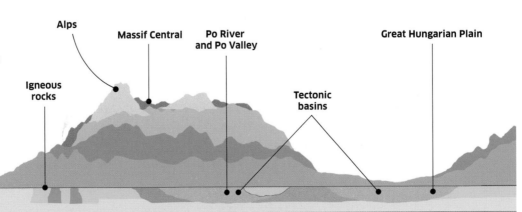

Alps

Massif Central

Po River and Po Valley

Great Hungarian Plain

Igneous rocks

Tectonic basins

Atlantic Ocean

THE ALPS

The Alps is the main mountain range of central Europe. These mountains stretch from Austria and Slovenia in the east, through Italy, Switzerland, Liechtenstein, and Germany to France in the west. With their snow-capped peaks, the Alps have been shaped by thousands of years of glacial erosion.

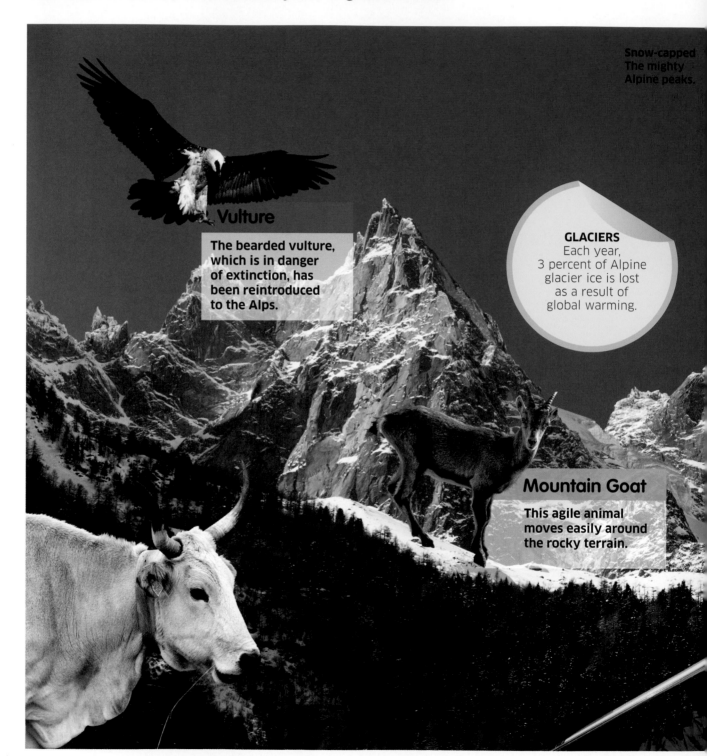

Snow-capped
The mighty Alpine peaks.

Vulture

The bearded vulture, which is in danger of extinction, has been reintroduced to the Alps.

GLACIERS
Each year, 3 percent of Alpine glacier ice is lost as a result of global warming.

Mountain Goat

This agile animal moves easily around the rocky terrain.

France

Mont Blanc is the highest mountain in the Alps. A 7-mile tunnel runs through the mountain.

Italy

This satellite view shows the Alps in Italy. The mountains cover an area of 115,830 square miles.

SIGHTS
DATA FILE

Facts about the Alps

The Alps is the longest mountain range in Europe. About 16 million people live in the Alpine region.

1. **Length of mountain range:** 746 miles
2. **Ecosystems:** Temperate deciduous forest, alpine pasture
3. **Highest peak:** Mont Blanc (15,781 feet)

Vacations

The slopes offer all kinds of activities, from mountaineering and hiking to snowboarding and skiing.

ITALY
DOLOMITES NATIONAL PARK

Typical Vegetation

The landscape of the Dolomites National Park is dominated by coniferous forests. About 1400 different species of plant grow in the park.

SNOW
SKIING SEASON

Lech–Zürs, Austria

One of Europe's most visited ski resorts, the area's steep slopes and snowy climate mean that its skiing season lasts from November to late April.

ÖTZI
THE ICE MAN

The Mummy and His Weapons

In 1991, the mummified body of a man was found in the ice on the border between Italy and Austria. The body was more than 5000 years old and had been preserved by the ice. The man has been named Ötzi the Ice Man. Next to his body lay his weapons: an ax, a knife, and a bow and arrows.

Studies suggest that Ötzi died during a fight.

THE DANUBE RIVER

Nearly 1800 miles long, the Danube is the second-longest river in Europe. The river supports many different industries, including tourism, fishing, and transportation.

60
out of 300
The number of the Danube's tributaries that are navigable.

MAJOR CITIES ON THE RIVER

Course

The Danube rises in the town of Donaueschingen in Germany's Black Forest. It flows from there to the Black Sea. The river passes through 10 countries: Germany, Austria, Hungary, Slovakia, Croatia, Serbia, Bulgaria, Romania, Moldova, and Ukraine.

POLLUTION
INDUSTRY

Chemicals

The Danube River flows through densely populated and industrialized areas, where there are **nuclear power** plants, factories, and farms. Many chemicals leak into the river, and its waters are badly polluted.

Fishermen

Fishing is an important industry on the Danube. This Romanian fisherman is holding two sturgeon that he caught in the river.

Suspension Bridge
A symbol of Budapest, in Hungary.

Budapest

This is a night scene of the Hungarian capital city, through which the river flows.

Danube Delta
About 15,000 people live in the Danube Delta, which is a UNESCO World Heritage Site.

Capital cities

The Danube is the only river in Europe to pass through four capital cities: Vienna, Bratislava, Budapest, and Belgrade.

Under Control
Dikes along the banks of the river stop it from flooding. There are also hydroelectric power plants built across the river to provide electricity.

Ships
The Danube is navigable by large ocean ships from the Black Sea to Brăila in Romania, and by smaller river ships to Kelheim, Bavaria, in Germany.

CLIMATE

Most of Europe has a temperate climate, but in the north and south, the temperatures can be more extreme. Countries to the west have mild climates that are moderated by the Atlantic Ocean. In the south, the Alps prevent cold winds from affecting the Mediterranean coast, where it can be very hot in summer.

Ice Floes in Norway
Ice floats in the sea off the coast of Spitsbergen Island, Norway. Temperatures there remain below 32 °F for most of the year.

STRONG WINDS
CANARY ISLANDS, SPAIN

The Sirocco

In the summer, a strong wind from North Africa blows across southern Europe. Called the Sirocco, it is a hot and dry wind that blows off the Sahara Desert. It sometimes carries thick clouds of sand, which can cause health problems, such as stinging eyes.

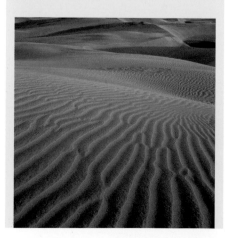

RAIN
LONDON, UNITED KINGDOM

Moderate Climate

The climate in London is moderate. During the summer, the average maximum temperature ranges between 70 °F and 75 °F. In the summer months, the city's many parks are full of people. Londoners make the most of the open spaces to exercise and picnic. The winter months are much colder, with temperatures dropping to 36 °F or lower. It can rain throughout the year in London, but rainfall is usually higher in the colder winter months. The annual average rainfall is about 23.6 inches.

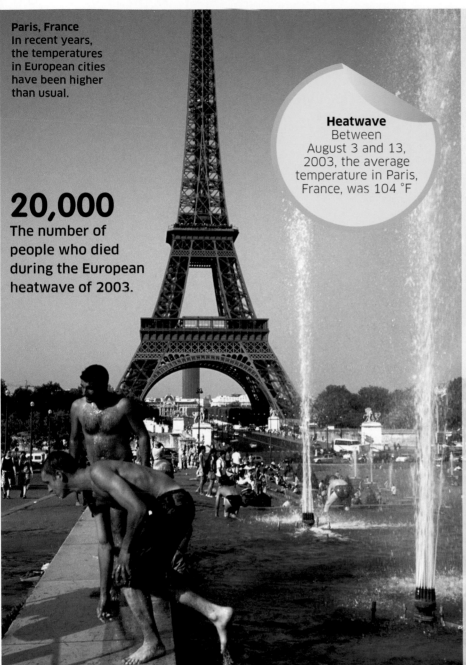

Paris, France
In recent years, the temperatures in European cities have been higher than usual.

20,000
The number of people who died during the European heatwave of 2003.

Heatwave
Between August 3 and 13, 2003, the average temperature in Paris, France, was 104 °F

HEATWAVE
CRISIS IN EUROPE

Consequences

In 2003, there was a **heatwave** throughout Europe. Southern countries, such as Spain, Italy, and Portugal, had the highest temperatures. Alicante in Spain saw temperatures reach 116.6 °F.

France

During the heatwave, temperatures in France reached their highest since 1950. In Paris, the temperature reached 104 °F during the day. The warmest night was on August 11–12, when the temperature only dropped to 78 °F.

Mediterranean

The climate of Portovenere, Italy (left), is extreme. The summers are often incredibly hot and the winters are very cold.

Greece

In winter on the Greek islands, it rains one day in three. However, the sea remains as warm as 59 °F even in the middle of winter.

THE DECIDUOUS FOREST HABITAT

Much of continental Europe is covered in temperate forests. These forests are home to deciduous trees such as oak, beech, and lime. Many animals, small and large, live in the forests, including squirrels, rabbits, wild boar, deer, foxes, eagle owls, and other birds of prey.

European green woodpecker

BUTTERFLIES
Caterpillars eat the tender leaves of oak and maple trees and many other plants. They then spin their cocoons on the trees before hatching as beautiful butterflies.

Brambling

Badger

Fallow deer
These well-camouflaged deer feed on grasses and acorns found on the forest floor. They live in herds of more than 100.

Red fox

Sheetweb spider

Sexton beetle
This beetle lays its eggs on the bodies of small animals. The larvae then feed on the bodies when they hatch.

Millipede

RECYCLING
Fungi play an important role in breaking down dead wood and other organic waste.

Earthworm

LEAF LITTER
Insects, fungi, and bacteria all play a role in breaking down the leaf litter. This important process provides the trees and other foliage with essential nutrients.

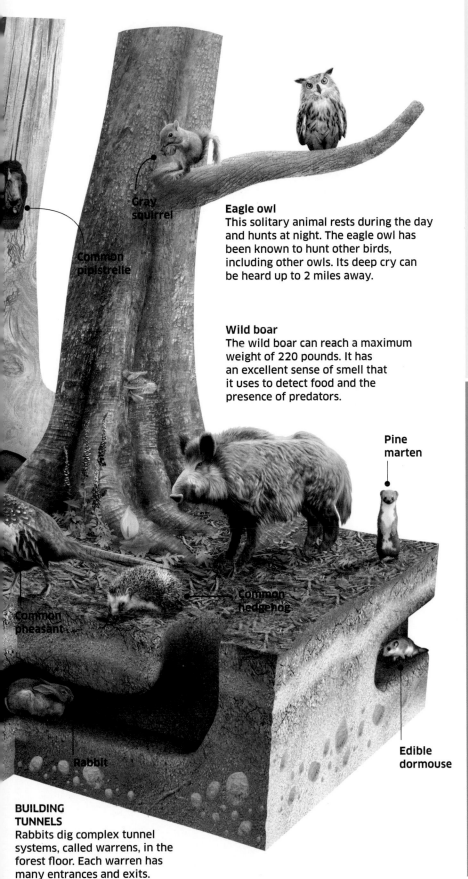

Eagle owl
This solitary animal rests during the day and hunts at night. The eagle owl has been known to hunt other birds, including other owls. Its deep cry can be heard up to 2 miles away.

Gray squirrel

Common pipistrelle

Wild boar
The wild boar can reach a maximum weight of 220 pounds. It has an excellent sense of smell that it uses to detect food and the presence of predators.

Pine marten

Common pheasant

Common hedgehog

Rabbit

Edible dormouse

BUILDING TUNNELS
Rabbits dig complex tunnel systems, called warrens, in the forest floor. Each warren has many entrances and exits.

LIFE IN THE WOOD

Hibernation
Many mammals, such as bats (below), sleep during the coldest weeks of winter. This is called hibernation. During hibernation, their body temperature and breathing are lower than normal. They use the fat reserves stored in their bodies during the warmer months, to survive the winter.

FALL DECIDUOUS TREES

Falling Leaves
During the fall months, the deciduous trees of Europe's forests lose their leaves. Fall starts in September. New leaves begin to grow in the spring, which starts in March.

Turning Brown
Plants need sunlight to produce the chlorophyll that keeps their leaves green. With less light in the fall, the trees stop producing chlorophyll and the leaves turn red, brown, and yellow.

POPULATION

In the 1900s, about 25 percent of the world's population lived in Europe. Today, the populations of other continents have grown to overtake Europe, but it is still a densely populated continent. It is mostly very developed, with modern cities and a high standard of living.

City of London
The City is London's financial district. It is lively and full of activity during the day, but much quieter at night.

LONDON, UNITED KINGDOM
A POPULOUS CITY

Business Center
London, the capital of the United Kingdom (UK), is home to about 7.83 million people. Built along the banks of the Thames River, it is a **cosmopolitan** city and world financial center.

Tower Bridge
This striking bridge opened in 1894. The bridge allows vehicles and pedestrians to cross from one side of the Thames River to the other. It also has an electrohydraulic system that enables it to open, to let ships and large vessels travel down the Thames.

Traditions
The UK has managed to balance modern living with the traditions of the past. As a result, the country has a rich and varied cultural heritage.

BELGIUM
BRUSSELS

Home of the European Union

Brussels is one of the most densely populated cities in Europe. The city is the capital of Belgium and also the administrative headquarters of the European Union (EU). Most of the city's inhabitants speak French, while some speak Flemish. The Royal Palace (below) was built in 1779 and is the official residence of the king of Belgium.

BULGARIA
JOINING THE EUROPEAN UNION

Between East and West

For many centuries, Bulgaria was ruled by the **Ottoman Empire**. After World War II, it was close to the Soviet Union. In January 2007, Bulgaria became a member of the **European Union**. The country's main ethnic groups are Bulgarians, Turks, and Roma. The photo below shows Nesebar, an old resort town on the Black Sea, and a peasant in traditional Bulgarian clothes.

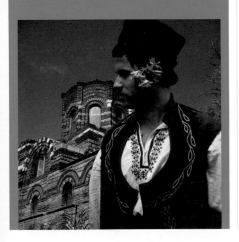

ITALY
NAPLES

Picturesque but Troubled

Naples, with about 1 million inhabitants, is the third-largest city in Italy. The city has beautiful historic buildings, but it is plagued by a high rate of unemployment and has a high crime rate.

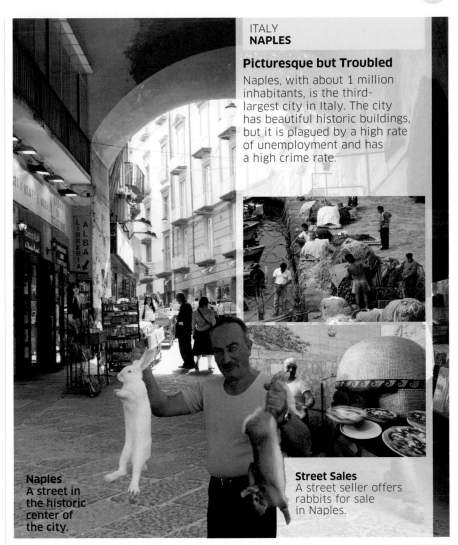

Naples
A street in the historic center of the city.

Street Sales
A street seller offers rabbits for sale in Naples.

RUSSIAN FEDERATION
MOSCOW

Biggest City

Moscow has over 11.5 million inhabitants, making it the largest city in Europe. Built along the banks of the Moskva River, it is the capital of the Russian Federation. The city contains many fine historical buildings, including the Kremlin (below), a huge fortified palace at the center of the city, which now serves as the official residency of the Russian president.

ECONOMY

Europe's economy is one of the strongest in the world. However, not all the countries in Europe share the same level of development—countries in the west tend to be more developed than those in the east. Trade, transportation, finance, tourism, and heavy industry drive the European economy.

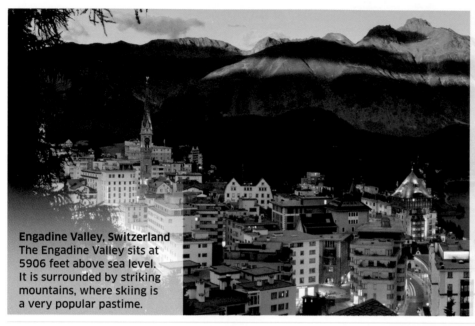

Engadine Valley, Switzerland
The Engadine Valley sits at 5906 feet above sea level. It is surrounded by striking mountains, where skiing is a very popular pastime.

ALPS
TOURISM

Snow Sports

Each year, snow sports attract millions of tourists to the Alps. These visitors provide the Alpine countries with a great economic boost.

Skiing
Skiers flock to the Alps.

TRANSPORTATION NETWORK
RAILROADS

High-Speed Trains

Despite its many natural borders, the European transportation network is highly developed. Due to the growth of trade with the East, the number of passengers and the volume of cargo coming into, and going out of, Europe has greatly increased. To solve the problem of congestion at airports and on highways, the continent has a network of high-speed trains that connects many of Europe's main cities in just a few hours. For example, it is possible to travel from London to Paris in about two hours.

CROPS
PRIMARY SECTOR

Bulgaria's Roses

Roses have been grown in Bulgaria's Rose Valley for centuries. The region is the leading producer of rose oil, which is used in perfumes. Collecting the roses is done by hand, usually by women.

The Eurostar
These trains travel between London, Paris, and Brussels.

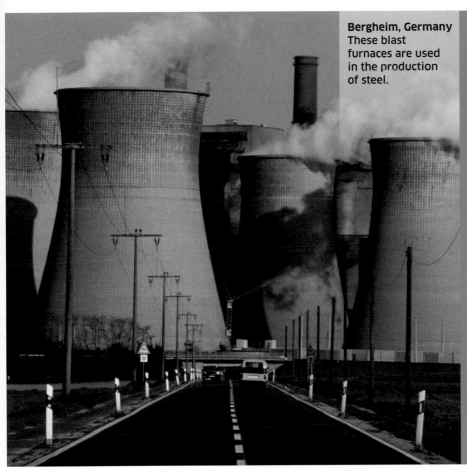

Bergheim, Germany
These blast furnaces are used in the production of steel.

NATURAL GAS

The Energy Problem
Most European countries have to **import** gas. Around 60 percent of Europe's gas is imported. Most comes from Russia. To avoid having to depend on Russia, many Western European countries are looking to use other energy sources, such as **solar**, wind, and nuclear **power**.

UNITY IN EUROPE

The European Union
Most of the countries in Europe belong to the European Union (EU). Citizens of EU countries can travel and work anywhere within the EU. Most of the countries use the euro as currency. As of 2012, the countries in the EU are: Austria, Belgium, Bulgaria, Cyprus, Czech Republic, Denmark, Estonia, Finland, France, Germany, Greece, Hungary, Ireland, Italy, Latvia, Lithuania, Luxembourg, Malta, Netherlands, Poland, Portugal, Romania, Slovakia, Slovenia, Spain, Sweden, and the United Kingdom.

Car factory
Germany, France, and Italy are the main car manufacturers in Europe.

POLDERS

Reclaiming Land
Polders are low-lying pieces of land that are enclosed by barriers called dikes that separate the land from the sea. Water is pumped out of the low-lying land, which dries up and can be used for farming. This technique was first used in the Netherlands in the twelfth century.

LANGUAGES AND PEOPLE

There are three main language groups in Europe: 300 million people speak Slavic languages, such as Russian and Polish, 200 million speak Romance languages, such as French, Italian, and Spanish; and another 200 million people speak Germanic languages, such as English, Swedish, and German.

Protected

Finnish, Hungarian, and Estonian are Uralic languages that are protected as national tongues. Other Uralic languages have been displaced by Russian.

Basque
Basque, spoken in parts of Spain and France, is the only European language that does not belong to the Indo-European group of languages.

Most Spoken

Due to European colonialism between the 16th and 20th centuries, English, Spanish, French, and Portuguese are among the most commonly spoken languages in the world.

Language
Speech is the most versatile form of communication.

Traditional Dress

There were 16 million Muslims living in the EU in 2007, and most are immigrants or the children of immigrants. Many Muslim women cover their heads with a traditional veil.

Immigrants

Immigrants in Europe face many kinds of discrimination. Here, demonstrators in London campaign against the deportation of Nigerian immigrants.

NATIVE LANGUAGES OF EUROPE

Indo-European languages

Almost all European languages are descended from Indo-European languages. These were spoken by Asiatic tribes that invaded Europe 6000 years ago. They gave rise to a number of language families:

❶ Albanian
❷ Baltic
❸ Celtic
❹ Slavic
❺ Germanic
❻ Greek
❼ Romance
❽ Uralic

Romance Languages

Descended from Latin, which was spread by the Roman Empire:

❶ Spanish, or Castilian
❷ Catalan
❸ French
❹ Portuguese
❺ Italian
❻ Romansh
❼ Romanian

Religion

The largest religious groups in Europe are Christian churches:

❶ **The Catholic Church**
Based around the absolute authority of the Pope.

❷ **Protestant Churches**
Anglicans, Calvinists, Lutherans, and others.

❸ **Greek and Russian Orthodox Churches**
Eastern European churches that do not recognize the authority of the Pope.

CASE STUDIES EUROPEAN IDENTITIES

AUSTRIA
AUSTRO-BAVARIAN

German Dialect

The Austro-Bavarian dialect is spoken in Austria and in the southern German state of Bavaria. This dialect is the native tongue of about 12 million people.

SCANDINAVIA
SAMI

Fight for Their Rights

The last aboriginal European culture still survives in remote parts of northern Scandinavia and Russia. The Sami—also known as Lapps—number about 80,000 people.

THE BALKANS
GREECE

Cradle of Civilization

Ancient Greece was one of the great civilizations of history. Today, modern Greeks consider themselves to be Western Europeans, although the country is located in the east of the continent.

ACROSS EUROPE
ROMA

Indian Peoples

Also known as gypsies, the **nomadic** Roma people arrived in Europe from India in the eleventh century. They number about 12 million people.

THE SAMI PEOPLE

The Sami people, or Lapps, are among the oldest inhabitants of Europe. Scattered throughout the **Scandinavian** countries, they total some 80,000 people. The Sami's traditional lifestyle changed first with the arrival of Christianity in the region 1000 years ago, then again with the technological advances of the twentieth century.

FROM AFRICA TO EURASIA

A Common Heritage

The first modern humans left Africa about 80,000 years ago and settled in Oceania and Asia. A second migration took place 35,000 years ago to the Middle East and the Balkans. It is thought that 80 percent of Europeans have **ancestors** who migrated at this time. It is thought that the other 20 percent of Europeans came from the Middle East about 10,000 years ago.

ADAPTATION TO THE CLIMATE

Fair Skin

It is thought that as people moved north from Africa to Europe, they had less exposure to the Sun. As a result, over time, their skin became lighter.

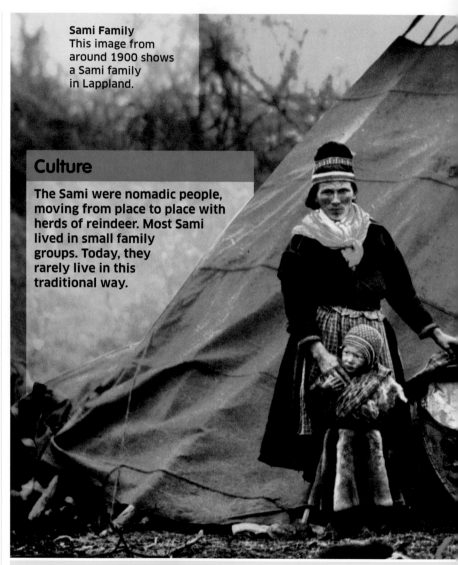

Sami Family
This image from around 1900 shows a Sami family in Lappland.

Culture

The Sami were nomadic people, moving from place to place with herds of reindeer. Most Sami lived in small family groups. Today, they rarely live in this traditional way.

Beliefs
The Sami religion focused on the worship of animal and ancestral spirits. Today, many are Christians and follow Lutheranism.

Tools

The Sami are skilled craftspeople who carve tools and other implements from bone, wood, antlers, and silver. Their carvings are often decorated with geometric patterns.

Identity

Although the Sami are spread across four countries (Norway, Sweden, Finland, and Russia), they have their own flag (left).

Tents

The tents used by the Sami were similar to North American tepees. They were made from reindeer skins and were easy to take down as the tribe moved from place to place. Today, most of the Sami live in European-style houses.

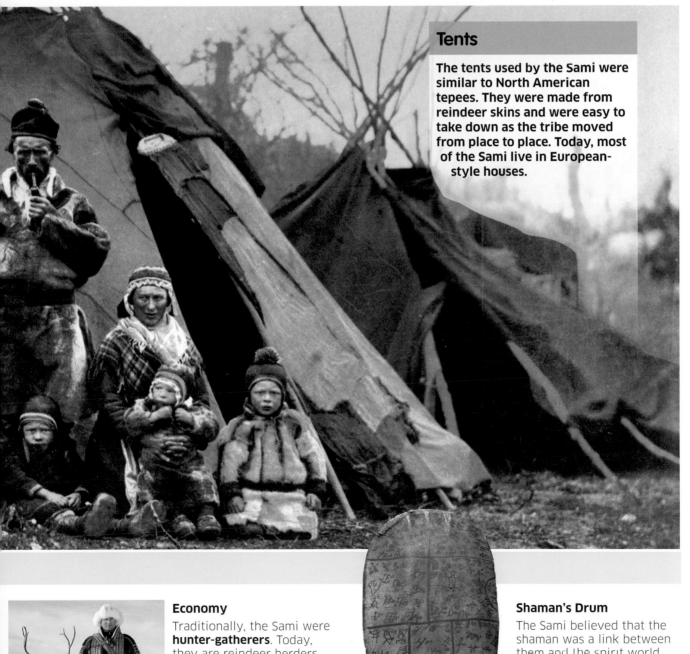

Economy

Traditionally, the Sami were **hunter-gatherers**. Today, they are reindeer herders, and they are thought to have about half a million reindeer.

Shaman's Drum

The Sami believed that the shaman was a link between them and the spirit world. During ceremonies, the shaman played a drum.

PRAGUE

Located in the heart of Europe, the Czech capital Prague has a rich musical tradition and was home to the famous composer Antonín Dvořák. The city has many tourist attractions, including museums, galleries, churches, synagogues, palaces, and gardens.

Country	Czech Republic
Area	191 sq mi
Population	1,258,106
Density	6587 people/sq mi

SYMBOLS OF THE CITY

Astronomical Clock

Prague's **astronomical clock** dates from the fifteenth century. It is one of the city's best-loved tourist attractions, and hundreds of visitors flock to stand under it each hour, waiting to see it working.

Charles Bridge

This famous bridge unites the old and new cities. It opened in 1503 and is 1693 feet long and 31 feet wide. There are religious statues along it, and those who stand on the bridge get a great view of Prague.

Population

According to 2006 data, 8.77 percent of the population of Prague was foreign-born.

Old Town Square

The Old Town Square is located between Wenceslas Square and Charles Bridge. The north side is dominated by the white facade of the church of Saint Nicholas. The Stone Bell House and the Goltz-Kinsky Palace are on the east side.

PEDESTRIANS

Many streets are pedestrianized. In summer, tables at the sidewalk cafes attract thousands of tourists.

Old Town

Prague's Old Town is free of traffic and surrounded by historic buildings.

TOURIST DESTINATION

Old Town

The first people to arrive in Prague settled in the Old Town. Among the highlights of the Old Town Square is the Astronomical Cock. Across the Vltava River lies the Lesser Town, which is known as Mala Strana in Czech.

Monument to Jan Hus.

Dancing House

This modern building in Prague is nicknamed "Ginger and Fred" after the US dancers Ginger Rogers and Fred Astaire. It is thought to look like a pair of dancers.

Vrtbovska Garden

Dating from 1720, this terraced garden has spectacular views of the city. Weddings, concerts, and other events are held in the garden.

THE COLOSSEUM

In the first century AD, the Colosseum was built in Rome by Emperor Vespasian. This **amphitheater** seated up to 50,000 spectators. Today, the ruins of the Colosseum are one of Rome's biggest tourist attractions.

THE COLOSSEUM
FACT FILE

Location:
Rome, Italy

Type:
Amphitheater

Date opened:
AD 80

Capacity:
50,000

Dimensions:

157 ft   617 ft   512 ft   1719 ft

Colossus

It is thought that the Colosseum was named after the colossal statue of Emperor Nero.

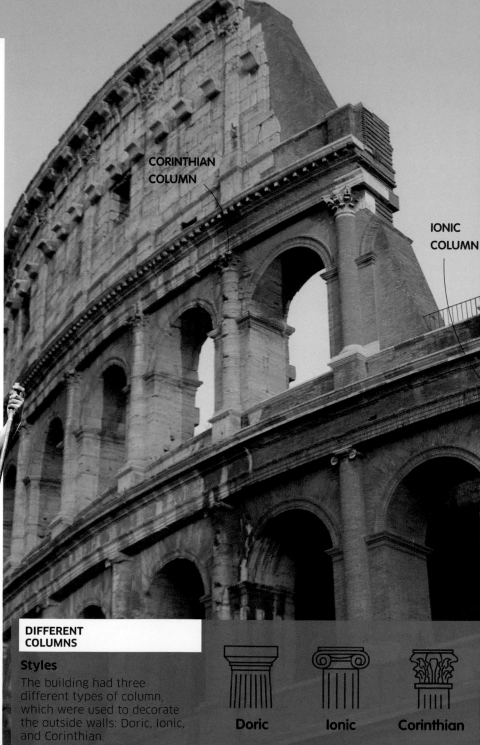

CORINTHIAN COLUMN

IONIC COLUMN

DIFFERENT COLUMNS

Styles

The building had three different types of column, which were used to decorate the outside walls: Doric, Ionic, and Corinthian.

Doric   Ionic   Corinthian

COLOSSEUM **UP CLOSE**

Sliding Roof
A canvas roof protected the public from rain and sun.

Underground
Cells and cages were built underground for the gladiators and wild animals.

Bleachers
Seating was arranged according to social class. The better seats were made from marble, while the top section was made of wood.

Arena
The Colosseum was used for bloody contests including mock sea battles, animal hunts, executions, and dramas based on mythology.

1 MILLION
The number of tons of stone and brick that were used to construct the arches.

Walls
They were raised with blocks of stone, brick, and **limestone**.

Ruins
After a series of earthquakes, much of the building has collapsed.

DORIC COLUMN

Colosseum
The outside view of the amphitheater.

THE ALHAMBRA

This walled city in southern Spain is a beautiful complex of palaces, forts, and gardens. It was home to the court of the Arab (Moorish) kingdom of Granada between the thirteenth and fifteenth centuries. The Alhambra is considered one of the greatest examples of Islamic art in Europe.

THE ALHAMBRA
FACT FILE

Date:
Ninth to fourteenth centuries

Location:
Granada, Spain

Structure:
Originally built for military purposes, the city was both a strong fortress and a palace. The Spanish added other buildings, such as the palace of Charles V.

10,000
The number of inscriptions that adorn the Alhambra.

JOINING THE SQUARES

Patio of the Lions

The garden displays the Muslim idea of Paradise. In each room, there are four waterfalls supported by 12 lions. The columns are joined with lace panels that let in sunlight.

Lion Fountain
Made from marble, this is found in the central courtyard.

Architectural Plan

1. Alcazaba
2. The Golden Room
3. Comares Palace
4. Palace of the Lions
5. Patio of the Lions
6. Palace of Charles V
7. Hall of the Kings
8. Monastery of St. Francis

Last King

Boabdil was the last king of Moorish Spain. He was overthrown in 1492 by Catholic forces from the north.

Motto

On many of the walls, the **inscriptions** read: "There is no god but Allah."

The Alhambra
View of the building in Granada, southern Spain.

Court of the Myrtles

When the Alhambra was built, water was in short supply, so the large pond here was a symbol of wealth and power. The court is also called the Court of the Pond.

Palace of Charles V

The palace was built in the sixteenth century. It is a **Renaissance**-style double-story building with a large, circular courtyard. Today, it houses the Museum of Fine Arts.

ASIA
INTRODUCTION

Asia makes up one-third of the Earth's continental landmass. The center of the continent is dominated by a large plateau and huge mountain ranges. Great rivers flow across Asia, including the Yangtze in China and the Ganges in India. The Earth's lowest place, the Dead Sea, can be found on the border of Israel and Jordan. The continent also has a great range of peoples. There are many different ethnic groups in Asia, from the Sherpas of the Himalayas, to the Roma. Each of them have their own beliefs, language, and lifestyle.

JORDAN
THE SANDSTONE IN THE REGION NEAR THE ANCIENT CITY OF PETRA IS CARVED INTO UNIQUE ROCK FORMATIONS, SUCH AS THESE CANYONS.

ASIA
PHYSICAL MAP

Aleutian Is.

BERING SEA

NORTH AMERICA

Bering Strait
Cape Dezhnev
Chukchi Peninsula
Anadyr
Anadyr Plateau

Wrangel Is.
Medvezhyi Is.
Novaya Sibir

EAST SIBERIAN SEA

New Siberian Islands
Kotelny Is.
Gt Lyakhovsky Is.

LAPTEV SEA

Komandorski Is.
Karaginsky Is.

Klyuchevskaya Sopka 15,584 ▲
SREDINNY RANGE
Shelikhov Gulf

Pobeda 10,325 ▲
KOLYMA MTS.

Kolyma
Indigirka
Yana
CHERSKY RANGE

VERKHOYANSK RANGE
Lena

Kamchatka Peninsula
C. Lopatka

Kuril Islands

SEA OF OKHOTSK

C. Elizabeth
Sakhalin
Tartar Strait
Amur
Shantar Is.

DZHUGDZHUR MTS.
GT KHINGAN RANGE
SIKHOTE-ALIN

Iturup
Kunashir

Hokkaido

SEA OF JAPAN

Honshu
Mt Fuji 12,388 ▲
Sumisu
Tori
Sofugan

Shikoku
Strait
KOREA
Bohai

MANCHURIA
YABLONOVYY RANGE

ARCTIC OCEAN

North Pole

160°
140°
120°
100°
80°
90°

160°
140°
120°
100°
80°

Taymyr Peninsula
Bolshevik Is.
Begichev Is.
BYRRANGA MTS.
Taymyr

Severnaya Zemlya
Komsomolets Is.
October Revolution Is.
C. Zhelaniya

KARA SEA

Bely Is.
L. Taymyr
Gydan Peninsula

Central Siberian Plateau

Kotuy

Lower Tunguska

Yenisey

SAYAN MTS.

S I B E R I A

L. Baikal

Mt Chajrchan Uul 14,193 ▲

GOBI DESERT

West Siberian Plain

Mt Belukha 14,783 ▲
ALTAI MTS.

Ob
L. Zaysan
L. Balkhash

Lenin Peak 23,406 ▲
TIEN SHAN

80°
60°
40°
20°

Franz Josef Land

Svalbard
20°

NORTH AMERICA

Novaya Zemlya

BARENTS SEA

Mt Narodnaya 6214 ▲
U R A L   M O U N T A I N S

Mt Yamantau 5381 ▲

ARAL SEA
Syr Darya
Amu Darya

EUROPE

Yamal Peninsula

70°

Arctic Circle

NORWEGIAN SEA

BALTIC SEA
NORTH SEA

Ural
Volga

Caspian Depression

CASPIAN SEA

Mt Damavand 18,389 ▲
ELBURZ MTS.
ZAGROS

60°

Sea of Azov

BLACK SEA
Bosphorus
Sea of Marmara
PONTIC MTS.
Anatolia
TAURUS MTS.
Cyprus
AEGEAN SEA

CAUCASUS
Mt Elbrus 18,510 ▲
Mt Ararat 16,946 ▲

Euphrates
SYRIAN DESERT
Tig

50°

Greenwich Meridian

NORTH ATLANTIC OCEAN

50°

Sinai Peninsula
MEDITERRANEAN SEA
Suez Canal

40°
30°

40°
30°

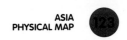
OCEAN

10°

0°

Islands

Talaud Is.

PHILIPPINE SEA

Halmahera

Philippines

20°

AUSTRALIA

30°

40°

130°

Samar

C. Engano

Leyte

Mindanao

CELEBES SEA

Maluku Islands

Seram

Buru

Sula

Sulawesi

Buton

Selayar

Timor

Taiwan

Luzon Strait

Babuyan Is.

Luzon

Mindoro

Panay

Negros

Sulu Arch.

Palawan

Spratly Is.

Flores

Sumba

Sumbawa

Taiwan Strait

Hainan

C. Baston

Parcel Is.

SOUTH CHINA SEA

Borneo

C. Puting

C. Selatan

Malay Archipelago

Bali

Java

Belitung

KEY

Altitude (in feet)

13,000 or over
6500
1600
650
0
−650 (depression)

Depth (in feet)

0
−650
−6500
−13,000
−19,500

120°

110°

Gulf of Tonkin

Mekong Delta

Con Son Is.

Natuna Is.

Bangka

Lingga Arch.

INDIAN OCEAN

Tropic of Cancer

Indochinese Peninsula

Mekong

Gulf of Thailand

C. Ca Mau

Sumatra

Enggano

100°

Salween

Isthmus of Kra

Strait of Malacca

Mergui Arch.

Phuket

Mentawai Islands

Nias

Siberut

Simeulue

90°

Brahmaputra

ANDAMAN SEA

HIMALAYAS

Mt. Everest
29,030

Gurla Mandhata
25,354

Andaman Islands

Nicobar Islands

80°

Ganges Delta

Bay of Bengal

Ganges

Sri Lanka

Pidurutalagala 6291

Indian Subcontinent

Yamuna

EASTERN GHATS

Godavari

Krishna

C. Dondra

70°

Narmada

WESTERN GHATS

C. Comorin

Lakshadweep Is.

Maldive Islands

Chagos Archipelago

Diego Garcia Is.

Indus

Gulf of Khambhat

60°

Gulf of Kutch

Indus Delta

ARABIAN SEA

INDIAN OCEAN

Gulf of Oman

C. Al Hadd

Masirah Is.

C. Madrakah

50°

Scale

1000 miles

Tropic of Capricorn

0

RUB' AL KHALI DESERT

Socotra

Gulf of Aden

AFRICA

Bab-al-Mandeb

40°

SEA

10°

0°

10°

20°

30°

40°

Equator

ASIA
POLITICAL MAP

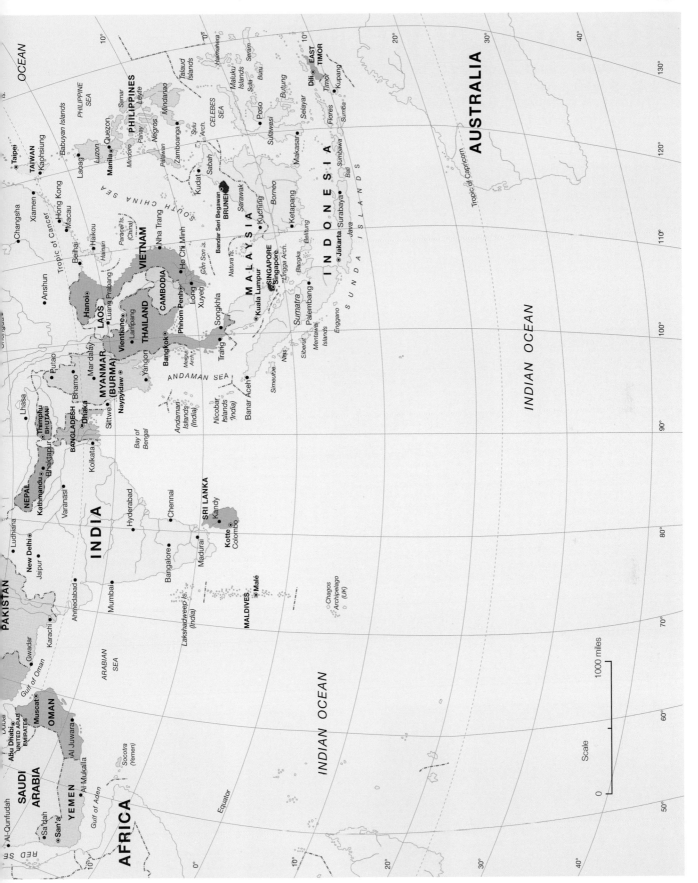

GEOGRAPHICAL WONDERS

Asia, the world's largest continent, has an enormous variety of landscapes. From some of the world's largest sandy deserts to crystal clear lakes and the highest summits in the world, it is truly a region of many contrasts.

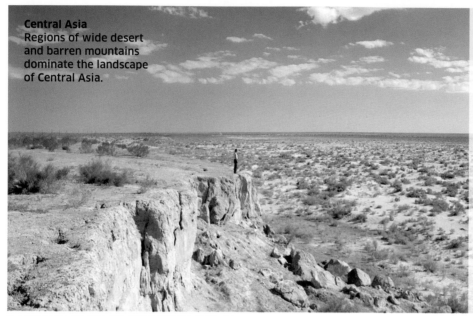

Central Asia
Regions of wide desert and barren mountains dominate the landscape of Central Asia.

TURAN AND KAZAKHSTAN
DESERTIFICATION

Dry Plateau

Central Asia is a region of hills, deserts, and plateaus. In the middle of Central Asia sits the Aral Sea, the world's fourth-largest saltwater lake. Since 1960, it has shrunk by almost 75 percent because the rivers feeding it were diverted to irrigate cotton fields. Poor vegetation combined with the region's dry climate—less than 15 inches of rain a year—have contributed to the spread of a process called desertification. This is when an area of desert begins to replace land that was previously **fertile**.

CENTRAL ASIA
ALTAI MOUNTAINS

Asia Gold Range

The Altai Mountains stretch across parts of Russia, China, Mongolia, and Kazakhstan. The mountains are separated by river valleys, which contain alpine meadows. The highest point is Mount Belukha (14,783 feet), on which there are several glaciers. The region is home to many diverse species, including the snow leopard.

CHINA
YANGTZE RIVER

Three Gorges Dam

The Yangtze River is the third-longest river in the world after the Nile and the Amazon. Its source is in Tibet and it flows for 3915 miles before reaching the Yellow Sea. In the final stretch of its upper course lies the Three Gorges Dam. A feat of engineering, this dam provides hydroelectric power to several large cities.

SAUDI ARABIA
DESERT SANDS

The Empty Quarter

South of the Arabian Peninsula is the Rub' al Khali Desert. The desert is one of the largest sandy deserts in the world and includes most of Saudi Arabia and areas of Oman, the United Arab Emirates, and Yemen, covering 250,966 square miles. It is known for its extreme weather conditions, making it virtually impossible to cross.

SIBERIA
LAKE BAIKAL

SOUTH-CENTRAL ASIA
THE HIMALAYAS

The Blue Eye of Siberia

Lake Baikal is known as the Blue Eye of Siberia because its waters are so clear and blue. Containing 20 percent of the world's fresh water, the lake is 395 miles long and 5315 feet deep. In 1996, the lake became a UNESCO World Heritage Site.

Olkhon island

The island of Olkhon (below) is 282 square miles, and is the largest island of Lake Baikal in eastern Siberia. The island is covered with forests and a small steppe, in addition to its own lakes.

The Himalayas is the world's highest mountain range. It is 1516 miles long. The range includes the formidable Mount Everest, which has a summit of 29,030 feet. The elevation of this mountain system is the result of a collision between the Indian and Eurasian tectonic plates, which began about 50 million years ago. The Himalayan region has many glaciers, which provide the area with a wealth of fresh water.

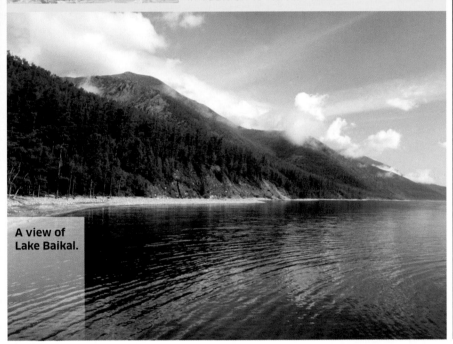

A view of Lake Baikal.

ASIAN RELIEF
ASIAN LANDSCAPE IN CROSS-SECTION

Asia has incredibly varied landscapes. As this cross-section shows, there are shields, deserts, plateaus, and basins.

The weight of the Tibetan Plateau contributes to the expansion of the Earth's crust to the east and west.

The expansion of the Earth's crust has caused faults across the Tibetan Plateau.

Arabian Shield

Persian Gulf

Iran Plateau

Thar Desert

Sichuan Basin

Lake Dongting

Earth's mantle

THE HIMALAYAS

The highest peaks on Earth, rising to over 29,000 feet, are found in this Asian mountain range. The Himalayan mountain range extends across several countries, including Pakistan, India, Nepal, Bhutan, and Tibet.

10,000
The number of attempts to climb Mount Everest in the last 50 years.

HIMALAYAN ORIGINS

Inhabitants of the Heights

The inhabitants of the Himalayas belong to many different peoples who belong to different religious groups. Mongolians, who follow Buddhism, are found mainly in the north. Muslims are found in the south, east, and west, with the center of the region dominated by Hindus.

The First

On May 29, 1953, New Zealander Edmund Hillary and his guide Tenzing Norgay (below) became the first people to reach the summit of Mount Everest. It is possible that the Englishman George Mallory succeeded in 1924, but he died during the descent.

HIMALAYAN RANGE
FACT FILE

Many Chains

The Himalayas is a system composed of numerous mountain ranges.

Area covered by the chain: 236,294 square miles

Ecosystem: High mountain

Maximum altitude: Mount Everest 29,030 feet

The Nearest Town

Muzaffarabad, the capital of Azad Kashmir, Pakistan, is located at the foot of the Himalayas. On October 8, 2005, a massive earthquake destroyed much of Muzaffarabad.

Flora

Firs, junipers (below), birch, and rhododendron plants are widespread throughout the area.

Lake Tsomgo
Located at 12,402 feet above sea level, Lake Tsomgo is 25 miles from Gangtok, the capital of the state of Sikkim. Although home to a variety of **fauna** and **flora**, the lake freezes over in the winter.

From Space
This satellite image shows the Himalayas as they look from space. The mountain range can be identified by the wrinkled appearance that it gives the Earth's surface.

RECORD
The Himalayan range has ten of the 14 highest peaks on Earth.

The Sherpas

The valleys of the Himalayas are inhabited by the Sherpas. These people are used to life in the mountains, and are often used as guides and escorts by mountaineers.

Mount Everest
The snowy peaks of the Himalayas rise high above the clouds.

MOUNT FUJI

This sacred mountain of Japan is a volcano that, while inactive for more than 300 years, is not extinct. It is considered to be the most perfect volcano on Earth because of the symmetry of its cone. At the base of Mount Fuji there are lakes, plateaus, waterfalls, and caves.

Blue and White

The blue and white flycatcher is a migratory bird. It breeds in Japan, Korea, and parts of China and Russia.

Spring

It is said to be spring in Japan when the cherry blossom tree comes into bloom.

TEMPERATURE
The lowest temperature ever recorded at Mount Fuji was -36 °F in February 1981.

Mount Fuji
Panoramic view of the volcano, the city Fujiyoshida, and Lake Kawaguchi.

Lake Kawaguchi
This lake is very famous because it reflects the north face of Mount Fuji like a mirror.

Sea of Trees
The forest *Aokigahara Jukai*, or Sea of Trees, is found on the ruins left by an eruption that took place in AD 864.

From Tokyo
In this aerial view of Tokyo, you can see Mount Fuji, a symbol of Japan, in the background.

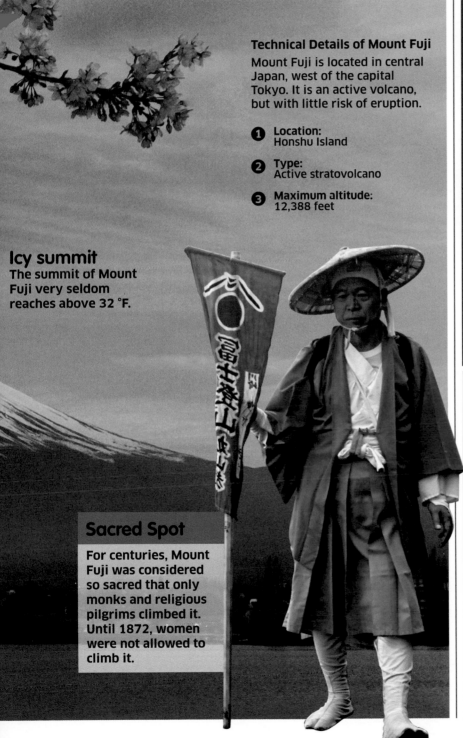

Technical Details of Mount Fuji
Mount Fuji is located in central Japan, west of the capital Tokyo. It is an active volcano, but with little risk of eruption.

1. **Location:** Honshu Island
2. **Type:** Active stratovolcano
3. **Maximum altitude:** 12,388 feet

Icy summit
The summit of Mount Fuji very seldom reaches above 32 °F.

Sacred Spot
For centuries, Mount Fuji was considered so sacred that only monks and religious pilgrims climbed it. Until 1872, women were not allowed to climb it.

HISTORY
THREE ERUPTIONS
Mount Fuji

There have been three major eruptions of Mount Fuji, with each one adding to the shape and size of the volcano.

700,000 years ago: Komitake eruption. Its summit today overlooks the eastern slope of Fuji.

100,000 years ago: several eruptions of the Old Fuji. This was then covered by several more eruptions.

December 1707: the last eruption.

Actual Fuji
Old Fuji
Ashitaka (first volcano)
Komitake

TOURIST INFORMATION

Shiraito Falls
Although this waterfall has a drop of only about 66 feet, it is a Japanese national monument and is sacred to the Japanese. The falls are surrounded by trees, making them an attractive tourist destination.

THE MONSOON

Monsoons are seasonal winds that bring rains. They govern the life and economy of one of the most densely populated regions of the world. The monsoon season begins with heavy rains, marking the end of the dry winter. Although people welcome the end of the winter, the monsoons can cause devastating floods that can destroy crops and homes.

ORIGIN
The word monsoon comes from the Arabic "mawsim," which means "season."

Benefits from Floods

Although the locals fear the flooding, the mud left by it increases soil fertility and ensures the health of future crops.

Crops in Oman
If monsoons do not destroy homes, they are welcomed by farmers because they make the soil more fertile, which leads to better crops.

Help from Other Countries
The devastating floods of 2010 left Pakistan reliant on help from other countries. Here, an observer in a military plane examines the scene of the floods.

2400
The number of deaths that occurred during the 2008 monsoon season.

Torrential Rains
In Vietnam, in September 2009, torrential rains left 300 people homeless. Eight people were killed in the torrential rains.

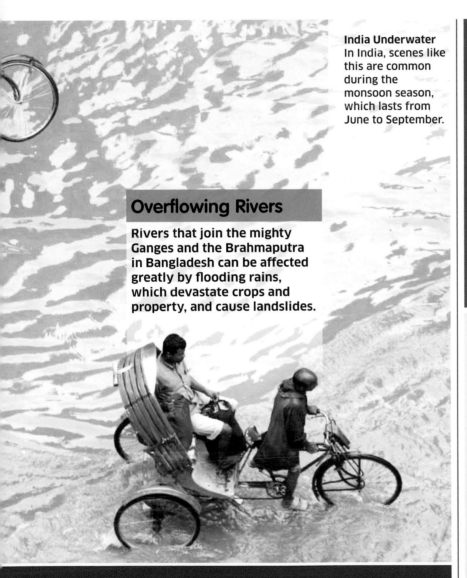

India Underwater
In India, scenes like this are common during the monsoon season, which lasts from June to September.

Overflowing Rivers
Rivers that join the mighty Ganges and the Brahmaputra in Bangladesh can be affected greatly by flooding rains, which devastate crops and property, and cause landslides.

HOW IT HAPPENS
MONSOON

Temperature Differences
Monsoons are seasonal winds that vary in direction according to the season. The winter monsoon is a cold wind blowing from the continent to the ocean. The summer monsoon blows from the Indian Ocean and South China Sea into Asia, dragging with it warm and humid air. This wind crashes into the high mountains and causes heavy rains between April and October. In recent years, as a result of global warming and climate change, the monsoons have grown in intensity.

ASIAN MONSOONS
PAKISTAN-LADAKH-CHINA-KOREA

Devastation in 2010
Floods in Asia devastated large areas. In Pakistan, more than 300,000 homes were damaged or destroyed. In the region of Ladakh, India, at least 185 people died. In China, there were more than 700 deaths, and in North Korea, 800,000 people had to leave their homes.

Disaster in Pakistan
This aerial view shows the 2010 flooding in Muzaffargarh, southern Punjab, Pakistan. Around 14 million people lost their homes in the flood.

THE GANGES RIVER

The Ganges River has its source in the Himalayas, at 13,583 feet. Along its 1557 miles course, it travels through mountains and plains to eventually empty into the Bay of Bengal. Civilizations have flourished on its banks, and today, cities, fertile rice paddies, and temples are found along its banks.

City of 1000 temples

The Vishwanath temple is the holiest in Varanasi. Dedicated to the god Shiva, it is covered with 1653 pounds of gold.

GANGES BASIN
FACT FILE

Symbol of Culture

The Ganges River is sacred to those who follow Hinduism. It also provides millions of people with fresh water.

Catchment area:
563,584 miles

Source of the river:
Gomukh at the mouth of Gangotri Glacier in the Himalayas

Length: 1557 miles

BELIEFS
RELIGIOUS CUSTOMS

The River is a Goddess

For Hindus, the Ganges is personified as the goddess Ganga. Hindus believe it is important for them to bathe in the river and for the ashes of their deceased loved ones to be scattered on its waters.

The Sacred River

The Ganges is sacred to followers of the Hindu religion. Its followers believe that the water of the river will save their souls. When Hindus die, they are **cremated** and their ashes are scattered in the river.

Varanasi, India
The city, seen from the river.

Contamination

Millions of people bathe in the Ganges River. All kinds of bacteria, sewage, and remains of cremations are found in the river, making it a source of contamination.

264 million

The number of gallons of sewage found along the course of the river.

140 MILLION

There are 140 million people living in the Ganges Delta.

Suspension Bridges

There are several bridges across the Ganges, including the Lakshman Jhula (which is older) and the Ram Jhula suspension bridges. They are designed only for pedestrians, but cyclists sometimes use them.

Calcutta (Kolkata)

With over 14 million inhabitants, Calcutta is one of the largest cities along the Ganges. During the colonial era, Great Britain ruled India. This building, dating from 1921, commemorates the British queen, Victoria.

ANIMALS OF THE GOBI DESERT

The Gobi Desert in northern China and southern Mongolia is extremely dry, especially during the winter. Extraordinary fossils have been found in the desert, which is home to camels, donkeys, wild horses, birds, and reptiles.

A COLD PLACE
The Gobi Desert is cold and there is often frost on the dunes.

Small Gobi

In the area of Small Gobi (*Alashan*) in Mongolia, migratory birds build their nests in small shrubs.

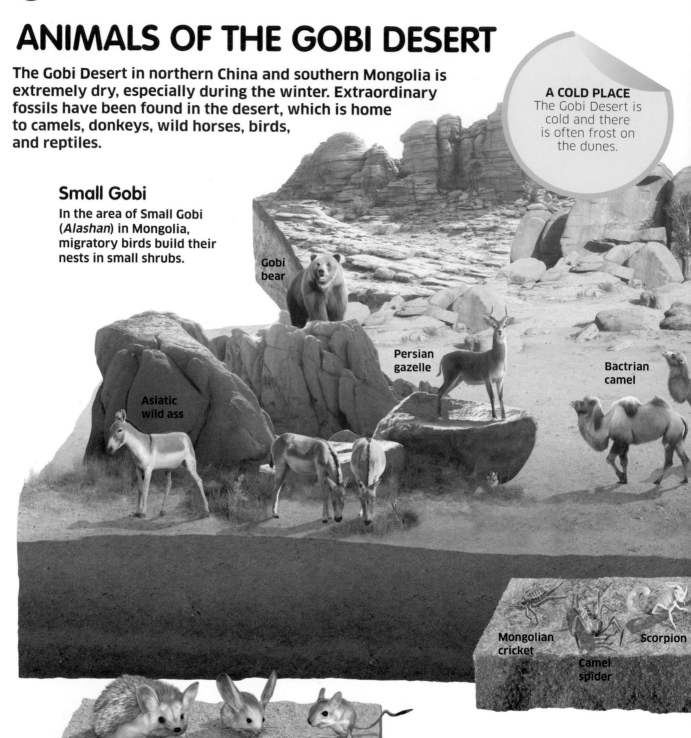

Gobi bear

Persian gazelle

Bactrian camel

Asiatic wild ass

Mongolian cricket

Scorpion

Camel spider

Long-eared hedgehog   Long-eared jerboa   Mongolian gerbil

Powerful Legs

The gerbil is active at night to avoid the high daytime temperatures. Gerbils use their strong hind legs and tails to leap in search of food, such as seeds.

Golden
eagle

Marsh
warbler

500,000
**The area in square
miles occupied by
the Gobi Desert.**

Wild Horses
**The wild horses of the Gobi
are known to have existed
for 20,000 years.**

Mongolian
wild horse

Tatar
sand
boa

Gobi gecko

Frog-eyed
gecko

Boa Constrictors
Tatar sand boas are found in the Gobi Desert.
These snakes hunt and kill their prey by
squeezing it until it suffocates. Once the prey
is dead, the snake then swallows it whole.

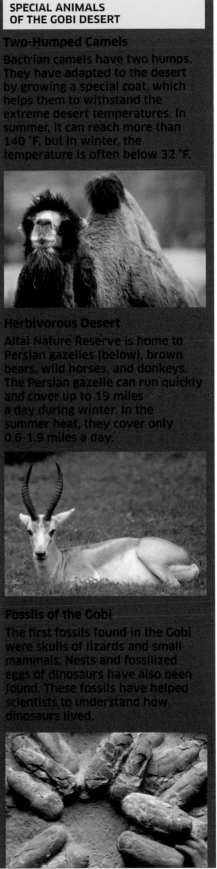

SPECIAL ANIMALS
OF THE GOBI DESERT

Two-Humped Camels
Bactrian camels have two humps.
They have adapted to the desert
by growing a special coat, which
helps them to withstand the
extreme desert temperatures. In
summer, it can reach more than
140 °F, but in winter, the
temperature is often below 32 °F.

Herbivorous Desert
Altai Nature Reserve is home to
Persian gazelles (below), brown
bears, wild horses, and donkeys.
The Persian gazelle can run quickly
and cover up to 19 miles
a day during winter. In the
summer heat, they cover only
0.6–1.9 miles a day.

Fossils of the Gobi
The first fossils found in the Gobi
were skulls of lizards and small
mammals. Nests and fossilized
eggs of dinosaurs have also been
found. These fossils have helped
scientists to understand how
dinosaurs lived.

POPULATION AND ECONOMY

Although Asia has more people than any other continent, its population is not evenly distributed. Large uninhabited areas contrast with some of the most densely populated areas on the planet. The economy has huge inequalities. There are massive contrasts between the rich oil-producing and industrialized countries, and the poverty of the countries in the central region.

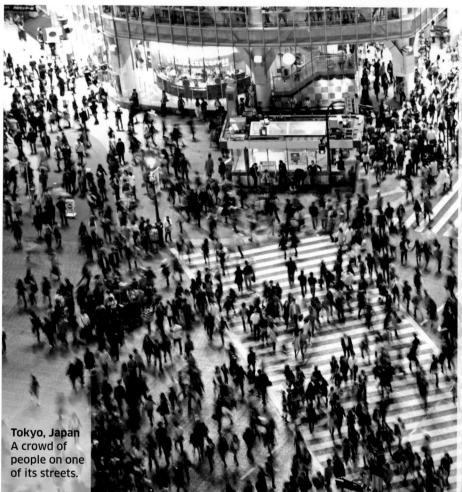

Tokyo, Japan
A crowd of people on one of its streets.

POPULATIONS
THE MOST POPULATED

Beijing, China
China's capital city, Beijing, is home to about 19.6 million people. Among its attractions are the palaces of the Forbidden City and part of the Great Wall of China.

Calcutta (Kolkata), India
The state capital of West Bengal, Calcutta has an urban area that is home to over 14 million people. Its official name is Kolkata, and until 1911, it was the capital of India.

Tourism
Asia has many places for visitors to see and tourism contributes handsomely to the economy. These camels are taking tourists to the ruins of Petra in Jordan.

Rice Paddies
Many Asian people still live in rural communities. Rice is the main agricultural product in Thailand. Rice grown there is exported around the world.

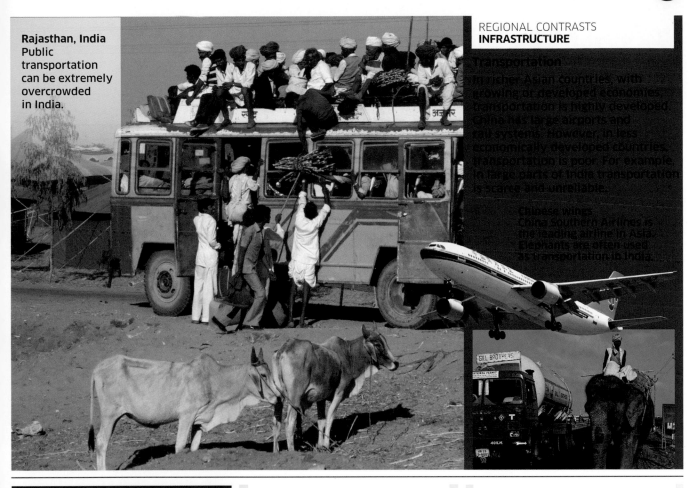

Rajasthan, India
Public transportation can be extremely overcrowded in India.

REGIONAL CONTRASTS
INFRASTRUCTURE

Transportation

In richer Asian countries, with growing or developed economies, transportation is highly developed. China has large airports and rail systems. However, in less economically developed countries, transportation is poor. For example, in large parts of India transportation is scarce and unreliable.

Chinese wings
China Southern Airlines is the leading airline in Asia. Elephants are often used as transportation in India.

Kuwait
Oil has made Kuwait one of the richest countries in the Arabian Peninsula.

HUMAN RIGHTS
CHILDREN

Poverty

Afghanistan, Bangladesh, Cambodia, and Laos are some of the poorest countries in Asia. With little economic development, people in these countries have a shorter than average life expectancy. In India and Southeast Asia, more than 30 million children are subjected to slave labor in exchange for food.

PANORAMA
LOCAL VERSUS EXPORT

Industry in Asia

China and Japan are seen as industrial powers. Many goods are made in China and Japan and exported to the West. While there is massive industrialization in parts of Asia, local industries, such as handmade textiles, are still important to some countries in Asia.

LANGUAGES AND PEOPLE

The size and diversity of the vast Asian continent mean that the people who live there are extremely varied. There are dozens of ethnic groups on the continent, and most groups speak their own language.

Hangul

North and South Korea have the same alphabet, called the Hangul. It is made up of 24 consonants and vowels.

Religions

Islam, Buddhism, and Hinduism are the main religions practiced by the people of Asia.

MOST SPOKEN
Mandarin Chinese is one of the most widely-spoken languages in the world.

Monks reading religious texts in Tibet.

Paper and Printing
Paper was invented in China in AD 104. Later, in the eleventh century, the Chinese were the first people to use a printing press.

Hebrew
The ancient language of Hebrew died in the first century AD. Nearly 2000 years later, it was revived and is spoken by almost all Israelis.

A COMPLEX HISTORY

Ancient Civilizations
Some of the oldest civilizations in the world flourished in Asia. For example:

1. **Sumer (3200–2300 BC):** This civilization grew in today's Iraq. The Sumerians developed writing and mathematics.
2. **China (united from 221 BC):** The Chinese Empire flourished until 1912.
3. **Harappa (2600–1800 BC):** In the northwest of India, they developed a system of writing.
4. **Persia (550 BC):** The Persian Empire was centered around present-day Iran.

Islamic Empires
After the rise of Islam, various empires formed:

1. **AD 630:** The tribes of the Arabian Peninsula were united in one state, which later expanded to include Syria, Palestine, and Africa.
2. **1200–1300:** The Mongols of Central Asia started to follow Islam and formed an empire that included China and India.
3. **1300:** West Asian Turks created the Ottoman Empire, which controlled a large area until 1923.

European Colonization
From the fifteenth century, the Portuguese began to trade and settle in parts of southern Asia. From the following century, the Dutch, English, and French controlled trading posts and entire countries, such as India and Indonesia.

MYANMAR
KAYAN

Long-Necked Women
Women of the Kayan people lengthen their necks by wearing long collars. With a population of just 130,000, the Kayan are one of Myanmar's ethnic minorities.

CHINA–VIETNAM–MYANMAR
MIAO

Living in the Mountains
There are 7 million Miao people. They are found in the mountain regions of China, Vietnam, and Myanmar. Their language is spoken in much of Southeast Asia.

FROM ASIA TO THE WORLD
ROMA

Mother and Daughter
The Roma can be traced back to northwestern India to the states of Punjab, Gujarat, Rajasthan, and Sindh (now Pakistan). Members of this group speak Romany.

INDIA
TODA

Pastoral People
Speaking a Dravidian language, this group lives in the Nilgiri Hills in southern India. They are shepherds and live in thatched houses built on wooden frames.

THE MONGOLS

Descended from the tribes led by Genghis Khan, the leader who conquered most of Eurasia in the early thirteenth century, the Mongols still live in the steppes of Asia, just as their ancestors did. Their lifestyle also remains largely unchanged and is still centered around their horses and grazing cattle.

FROM ASIA
THE BERING STRAIT

Across Continents
Around 15,000–30,000 years ago, the Earth was approaching the end of the last glaciation. During this time, large numbers of people migrated from eastern Asia to North America. Some scientists believe that this crossing was via the Bering Strait, which at that time was frozen, allowing the people to cross from Asia to North America.

A LARGE FAMILY

Asian and North American

Most scientists believe that the ancient Asians (their descendants are pictured below) who now inhabit southern Siberia are related to today's Native Americans.

Lunar New Year

Mongolians celebrate New Year according to the old **lunar calendar**. The festival is celebrated for three days in late January. People entertain guests and cook special food.

Traditional Houses

Many Mongolians still live in large tents called yurts. The tents are easily transportable and suit the Mongolians' nomadic way of life.

Nomadic Economy

Cattle give the Mongolians food in the form of meat and milk, transportation, and skins. Families travel great distances to find food for their cattle.

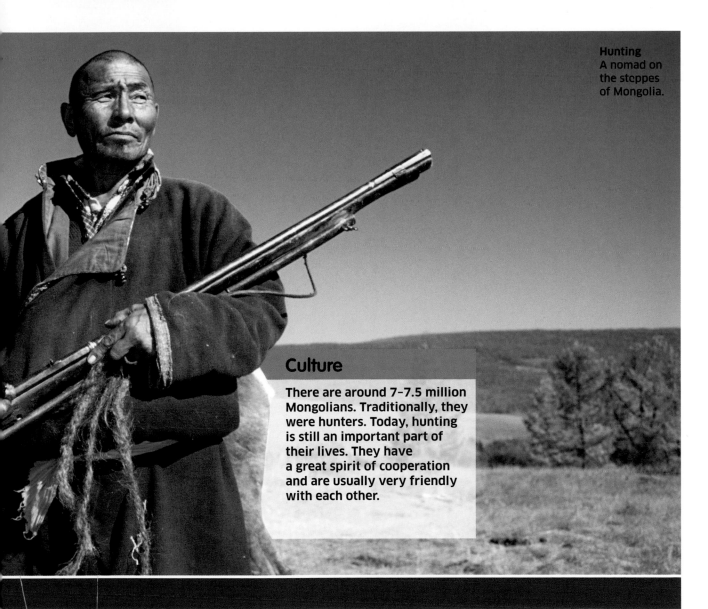

Hunting
A nomad on the steppes of Mongolia.

Culture

There are around 7–7.5 million Mongolians. Traditionally, they were hunters. Today, hunting is still an important part of their lives. They have a great spirit of cooperation and are usually very friendly with each other.

Beliefs

The Mongolian people have built shrines from rocks or wood, called oboo, in which they believe local spirits and gods live. Shrines usually face south or southeast.

Mongolian Song and Dance

Mongolians perform the *tsam*—a traditional masked dance to exorcize evil spirits. Mongolians play music on a variety of instruments and sing traditional songs.

THE TAJ MAHAL

The Taj Mahal is a beautiful mausoleum, or tomb, next to the Yamuna River in the Indian city of Agra. It was built in the seventeenth century by the Mogul emperor Shah Jahan to honor his wife, Mumtaz Mahal, who had died in childbirth. They are now both buried in this sparkling mausoleum built of white marble with precious stones laid into it.

THE TAJ MAHAL
FACT FILE

Location:
Agra, India

Type
Mausoleum

Built:
Between 1631 and 1654

Commissioned by:
Emperor Shah Jahan,
the Mogul Dynasty

Height:
243 feet

Construction:
43 types of marble
and precious stones
(turquoise, agate,
lapis, coral, jade,
and malachite)

Symmetry
The palace was located at the bottom of the field, behind the fountains and gardens. This meant that nothing obstructed the view of the **mausoleum**.

LIGHT
The precious stones embedded in the marble sparkle in the light, giving color to the marble.

1 Royal tomb
2 Mosque
3 Jawab
4 Canal
5 Palace gardens
6 Grand entrance

TAJ MAHAL **DETAILS**

Arches
The arches of each doorway give depth to the structure and reflect sunlight.

Lattices
Filigree railings surround the area of the royal tombs.

Borders
Drawing and verses from the Koran have been used to add decoration.

Onion-shaped dome
Domes of this shape are typical of Islamic architecture.

Minarets

Plinth
The mausoleum sits on a plinth. It adds height to the building, making it look more impressive.

Minarets

The tomb is surrounded by four towers, or minarets, one at each corner of the base. Faithful Muslims are called to prayer from the minarets.

22
The number of small domes symbolize the years of work.

Gardens
The gardens are divided into 16 sections, with many beds of flowers, raised paths, rows of trees, fountains, streams, and wide ponds. The water reflects the majestic palace.

DETAIL
THE TOMBS

Features
Made of marble decorated with rhinestones, the tombs are found in the main building. They are decorated by a ring of lotus flowers. This decoration is repeated on each minaret.

Shah Jahan

Mumtaz Mahal

Burial Chamber
The tombs of the couple are found in the central hall of the mausoleum.

BEIJING

The People's Republic of China's capital city, Beijing, is one of the world's most densely populated cities. The city is a mix of the ultramodern and the ancient, with skyscrapers and office towers sitting alongside ancient palaces, temples, and plazas.

Dashalar
A view of this bustling shopping center, just south of Tiananmen Square.

Country	China
Area	6487 sq mi
Population	19,612,000
Density	3023 people/sq mi

CITY ICONS

Temple of Heaven

This round temple complex is typical of the buildings of the Ming Dynasty. Each morning in the temple grounds, people practice t'ai chi and qigong.

Tiananmen Square

Surrounded by public buildings, this is a large square in the center of Beijing. It is the third largest public square in the world and has been the site of many events in Chinese history.

Dragon
The dragon is a symbol of force and power in Chinese culture.

SHOPPING
In this shopping avenue, shoppers can find everything, from modern jewelry and designer clothes, to traditional healers and medicines.

Entrance to Dashalar

Dashalar is a shopping avenue with more than 580 years of history. This bustling area gives an indication of what the ancient city of Beijing was like.

Transportation

The city has a wide range of public transportation that includes a subway, trains, buses, trams, and airplanes. The image on the left shows Beijing Central Station.

Beijing National Stadium

The 2008 Olympic Stadium has been nicknamed the "bird's nest" because of the intricate network of steel on its outside. The stadium is 1083 feet long, 722 feet wide, and 226 feet high.

CULTURAL EXPRESSIONS

National Grand Theater

This building was designed by Paul Andreu and resembles an egg cut in half. The lagoon it rests on reflects the other half to make a complete oval. The theater offers drama, dance, and opera.

Beijing Opera
The Beijing Opera has two centuries of history. It is considered one of the highest forms of Chinese culture.

Population

Including the greater metropolitan area, the Beijing population is expected to reach 20 million by 2020.

THE FORBIDDEN CITY

Building of the Forbidden City in Beijing, China, began in 1406 during the Ming Dynasty. The city, with nearly 1000 buildings, took 14 years to complete. It was home to 24 emperors.

View of the museum Beijing, China.

Roofs
Pottery figurines of dragons and winged lions protect the Forbidden City from evil spirits.

THE FORBIDDEN CITY
FACT FILE

Date of construction:
1406–1420

Location:
Beijing, China

Features:
Covering 861,110 square feet, the city is surrounded by a moat that is 20 feet deep. Its thick walls are capable of withstanding gunfire.

EXTREME SECURITY

Defense of the City
In addition to its thick walls and surrounding moat, the city has watchtowers at each of its corners. It was called Forbidden City, because no one was allowed to enter or leave the city without permission from the emperor.

Sahumadores

The palaces and courtyards had beautiful perfume burners, which spread a cloud of scent during ceremonies.

Ornamentation
Most of the buildings were built of wood. The ceilings have fine woodworked details on their eaves and numerous decorative pieces.

Perfect Harmony
The Hall of Harmony is perfectly **symmetrical**. Here, the emperor would rest and receive tributes from the ministers. The hall was also used for large celebrations.

9000
The number of rooms in the Forbidden City.

Perpetual Harmony
Here, the emperor received foreign rulers. Its name was inspired by the teachings of the Chinese philosopher Confucius.

Supreme Harmony
This is the most important room. It is 123 feet high with a marble base and six columns.

Perfect Harmony
See the box at the top of the page.

The Dragon Throne
This throne was used only on the emperor's birthday, for New Year celebrations, and the beginning of a war.

AFRICA
INTRODUCTION

Africa's landscapes range from dry, scorching deserts to lush jungles and to the snow-capped peak of Mount Kilimanjaro. While water is scarce throughout much of the continent, the Nile River provides water and fertile land. The African plains are dry and hot, but are also home to huge herds of grassland animals and their hunters. These animals range from elephants and lions to smaller creatures, such as baboons and antelope.

MADAGASCAR
THE ISLAND OF MADAGASCAR LIES JUST OFF THE COAST OF MOZAMBIQUE. THIS VOLCANIC CONE IS NEAR LAKE ITASY.

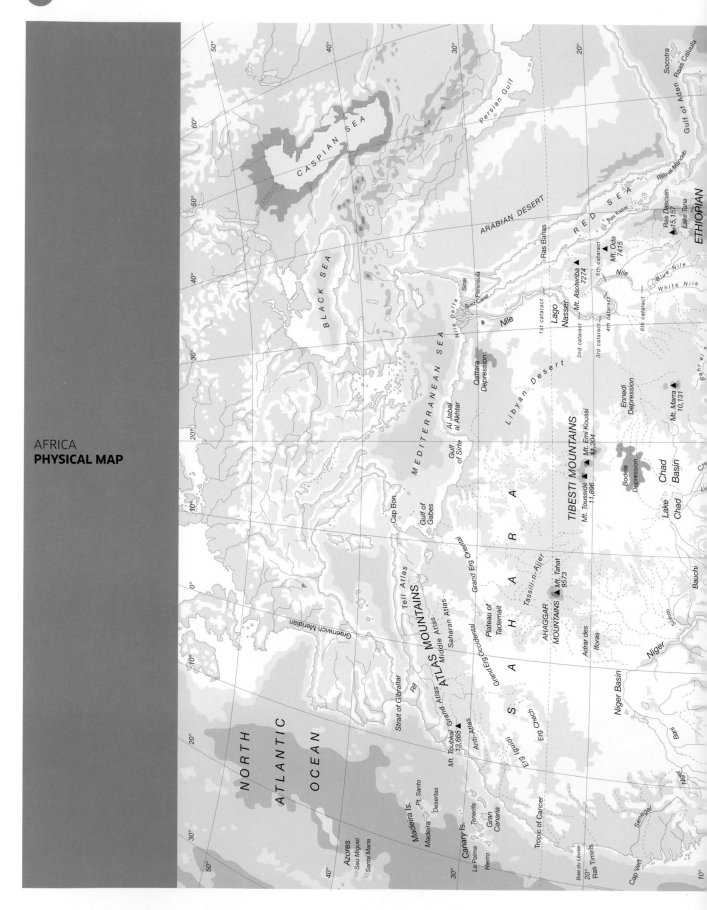

AFRICA
PHYSICAL MAP

CASPIAN SEA

Persian Gulf

ARABIAN DESERT

Gulf of Aden

Socotra

Raas Caluula

Bāb-al-Mandeb

RED SEA

Ras Dascian
15,157
Lake Tana

ETHIOPIAN

Ras Kasar

Mt. Oda
7415

Mt. Asoteriba
7274

5th cataract

Blue Nile

White Nile

Nile

4th cataract

6th cataract

Ras Banas

BLACK SEA

Sinai

Suez Canal

Nile Delta

Nile

1st cataract

Lago
Nasser

2nd cataract

3rd cataract

Bahr el

Qattara
Depression

MEDITERRANEAN SEA

Al Jabal
al Akhtar

Libyan Desert

Ennedi
Depression

Mt. Marra
10,131

Gulf
of Sirte

TIBESTI MOUNTAINS

Mt. Emi Koussi
11,204

Bodélé
Depression

Chad
Basin

Ch

Cap Bon

Gulf of
Gabes

Mt. Toussidé
11,896

Lake
Chad

S
A
H
A
R
A

Tell Atlas

ATLAS MOUNTAINS

Middle Atlas

Saharan Atlas

Grand Erg Oriental

Plateau of
Tademait

Tassili-n-Ajjer

Mt. Tahat
9573

AHAGGAR
MOUNTAINS

Adrar des
Iforas

Bauchi

Greenwich Meridian

Rif

Grand Atlas

Anti-Atlas

Mt. Toubkal
13,665

Grand Erg Occidental

Erg Iguidi

Erg Chech

Niger

Sokoto

Niger

NORTH

ATLANTIC

OCEAN

Strait of Gibraltar

Niger Basin

Bani

Madeira Is.

Pt. Santo

Desertas

Madeira

Azores

Sau Miguel

Santa Maria

Canary Is.

Tenerife

La Palma

Hierro

Gran
Canaria

Tropic of Cancer

Erg Timtint

Baie du Lévrier

Ras Timiris

Cap Vert

Senegal

Niger

KEY

Altitude (in feet)

13,000 and over
6500
1600
650
0
-650 (depression)

Depth (in feet)

0
-650
-6500
-13,000
-19,500

INDIAN OCEAN

Mascarenhas Is.

C. Masoala

Mt. Tsaratanana 9469

C. d'Ambre

Farquhar Is.

Isles Glorieuses

Cosmoledo Atoll

Aldabra Is

Mt. Tsiafajavona 8655

Madagascar

Cap Sainte-Marie

Mozambique Channel

C. Delgado

Njazidja

Mwali

Nzwani

Mayotte

Pemba

Zanzibar

Giuba

Turkana

Mt. Kenya 17,063

L. Kyoga

Lake Albert

Mt. Ruwenzori 16,794

Lake Victoria

L. Edward

Lake Kivu

Mt. Kilimanjaro 19,340

Mt. Rungwe 10,482

Lake Rukwa

Lake Tanganyika

Ruvu

Ruvuma

Rufiji

Shire

Lake Nyasa

Mount Nyanga 8514

Bight of Sofala

Delagoa Bay

Congo

Congo Basin

Lualaba

Lomami

Sankuru

Lake Mweru

Lake Bangweulu

Lake Mai-Ndombe

Kasai

Kwilu

Kasai

Lulua

Zambeze

Kafue

Lake Kariba

Zambeze

Victoria Falls

Cuando

Lunda Plateau

Culto

Cubango

Okavango Delta

Makgadikgadi

KALAHARI DESERT

Limpopo

Orange

Vaal

Thabana Ntlenyana 8143

DRAKENSBERG

Cape Agulhas

Cape of Good Hope

False Bay

St Helena Bay

NAMIB DESERT

Brandberg 8550

Etosha Pan

Cunene

Walvis Bay

Cape Fria

Mount Moco 8596

Benguela

Cuango

Quango

Sanga

Ogôoué

Cap Lopez

Bight of Biafra

Principe

São Tomé

Gulf of Guinea

SOUTH

ATLANTIC

OCEAN

Tropic of Capricorn

Equator

Ascension Island

Congo (Zaïre)

INDIAN OCEAN

Prince Edward Island

Marion

Scale

300 miles

0

Cape Verde Islands

Santo Antão
São Vicente
Santa Luzia
São Nicolau
Sal
Boa Vista
Maio
Santiago
Brava
Fogo

25°
15°
10°
25°

Seychelles

Amirantes Is.
Platte
Coetivy
Cerf
Farquhar

55°
10°
55°

Mascarenhas Islands

Mauritius
Réunion

Madagascar

Tropic of Capricorn

INDIAN OCEAN

60°
20°
60°

AFRICA
POLITICAL MAP

Gulf of Guinea

(Equatorial Guinea)
Bata
EQUATORIAL GUINEA
SÃO TOMÉ
AND PRÍNCIPE São Tomé
São Tomé

Ebolowa
Libreville
Booué
GABON
Port-Gentil
Tchibanga
Cabinda

CONGO
Brazzaville
Ouesso
Matadi
Kinshasa
Uige
Ambriz

Luanda
Porto Amboim
Cambundi
Benguela

ANGOLA
Namibes
Tômbua

UGANDA
Arua
Watsa
Kisangani
Kasese
Goma
Djolu
Boende
Ilebo
Feshi

DEMOCRATIC
REPUBLIC OF
THE CONGO
Kananga
Kamina
Kabinda
Saurimo
Dilolo
Sousa
Cambundi

KENYA
Mogadishu
Merca
Kismayu
Garissa
Lamu
Kisumu
Nairobi
Mombasa
Kampala
Voi
Tanga

RWANDA
Kigali
Bujumbura
BURUNDI

TANZANIA
Mwanza
Tabora
Dodoma
Karema
Mbala
Moba

ZAMBIA
Lubumbashi
Lusaka
Ndola
Livingstone
Hwange

Livingstonia
Tete

MALAWI
Lilongwe
Songea
Lichinga

MOZAMBIQUE
Nampula
Vila de Mocuba
Beira
Nova Mambone
Inhambane
Chicualacuala
Maputo

Dar es Salaam
Kilwa

SEYCHELLES
Cosmoledo
(Seychelles)
Aldabra Is.
(Seychelles)
Glorieuses Is.
(France)
Moroni
COMOROS

MADAGASCAR
St-Denis
Réunion
(France)
Antsiranana
Antalaha
Mananara
Tamboborano
Antananarivo
Morondava
Farafangana
Androka
Tolanaro

ZIMBABWE
Harare
Mazunga
Polokwane

BOTSWANA
Francistown
Molepolole
Gaborone

NAMIBIA
Windhoek
Mariental
Opuwo
Grootfontein
Lüderitz
Port Nolloth
Bitterfontein

SOUTH
AFRICA
Pretoria
Johannesburg
Bloemfontein
SWAZILAND
Mbabane
Maseru
LESOTHO
Durban
Mthatha
East London
Port Elizabeth
Cape Town

Prince Edward
Islands
(South Africa)

INDIAN OCEAN

SOUTH ATLANTIC OCEAN

Tropic of Capricorn

Mozambique Channel

CAPE VERDE
Santo Antão Is.
São Vicente Is.
Santa Luzia Is.
São Nicolau Is.
Sal Is.
Boa
Vista Is.
Maio Is.
Cape Verde
Archipelago
Santiago Is.
Praia
Fogo Is.
Brava Is.
Ascencion Is.
(UK)

SEYCHELLES
Victoria
Platte Is.
Coëtivy Is.
Amirante
Islands
Seychelles
Archipelago
Cerf Is.
Farquhar Atoll

MAURITIUS
Mascarene Islands
Port Louis
Mauritius
Réunion Is.
(France)
Madagascar
INDIAN OCEAN

Equator

600 miles

Scale

0

GEOGRAPHICAL WONDERS

As a result of wind and water erosion, plateaus dominate the African landscape. The northern region is home to the Atlas Mountains. In the eastern region, the Great Rift Valley divides Africa from north to south.

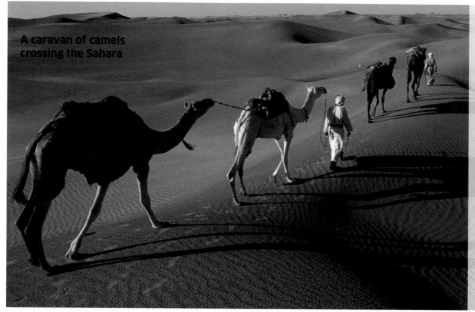

A caravan of camels crossing the Sahara

SAHARA
THE WORLD'S LARGEST DESERT

Temperature

The Sahara is the world's biggest desert extending nearly 3.47 million square miles. Mountains, including the Ahaggar Mountains in southern Algeria (which have peaks of up to 9843 feet high), interrupt the desert landscape. The difference in temperature varies greatly between day and night. During the day, the temperature can reach above 122 °F; but at night it can drop to 32 °F.

TUNISIA–ALGERIA–MOROCCO
MOUNTAIN RANGES

Atlas Mountains

With peaks reaching more than 13,123 feet, the Atlas Mountains in North Africa feature some of the highest peaks on the continent. The mountains run from east to west over 932 miles and cross three countries.

ZAMBIA–ZIMBABWE
ZAMBEZI RIVER

Kariba Dam

In Africa, there are more than 1200 dams. Like the Kariba Dam, most of them were built as a solution to problems such as drought. Building these dams has caused serious damage to ecosystems and has led to a massive displacement of people.

DJIBOUTI–MOZAMBIQUE
GEOLOGICAL FRACTURE

Rift Valley

The Great Rift Valley is one of Africa's most important geographical features. It was formed 20–25 million years ago, when the Earth's crust broke along a stretch of weakness. It extends from western Asia to southeastern Africa.

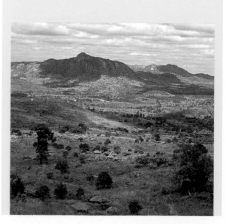

KENYA
VOLCANIC MOUNTAINS

The Last Glaciers

There are only three glaciers left in Africa: Mount Kilimanjaro, Mount Kenya (left), which are both of volcanic origin, and Rwenzori Mountains. With the rapid increase in global warming, these glaciers are in serious danger of disappearing.

Old Volcano

Mount Kenya was covered by ice for thousands of years. This has resulted in a badly eroded hillside and numerous valleys. It is now made up of 11 small glaciers.

Mount Kilimanjaro
An icy summit contrasts with the surrounding landscape.

ZAMBIA–ZIMBABWE
VICTORIA FALLS

Waterfalls

The Victoria Falls are located on the border between Zambia and Zimbabwe. The Falls are neither the world's highest nor widest. However, their height of 328 feet and their width of 5577 feet combined, make them the mightiest in the world. The Falls have been declared a World Heritage Site by UNESCO.

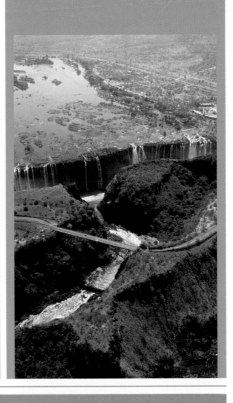

PROFILE
THE AFRICAN CONTINENT

This cross-section, from northwest to southeast, shows the great contrasts in the continent's relief.

19,340 FT
The height of Mount Kilimanjaro, Africa's highest mountain.

Atlas Range · Ahaggar Mountains · Lake Chad Basin · Congo Basin · Huila Plateau · Kalahari Basin · Drakensberg Mountains · Highveld

MOUNT KILIMANJARO

Africa's tallest mountain is a huge volcano that rises 19,340 feet above sea level. Although Mount Kilimanjaro is only 205 miles south of the equator, its summit remains covered with a layer of **permafrost**. The last volcanic activity on the mountain was just 200 years ago.

Elephants
Elephants, buffaloes and giraffes can be found on the surrounding plains.

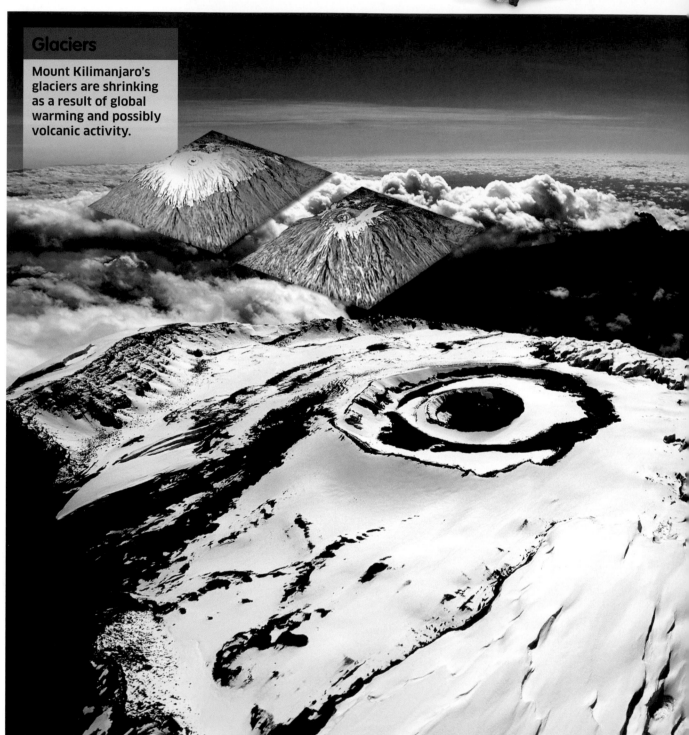

Glaciers
Mount Kilimanjaro's glaciers are shrinking as a result of global warming and possibly volcanic activity.

Three in One

Kilimanjaro has three craters: Kibo, Mawenzi, and Shira. Mount Meru, in the Monduli Mountains, and Ngurdoto Crater lie to the west.

CRATERS OF KILIMANJARO

Monduli Mountains | Mount Meru | Ngurdoto Crater | Shira | Kibo | Mawensi

Technical Data

Kilimanjaro is a stratovolcano located in Tanzania, East Africa.

① **Geological system:** the Great Rift Valley which crosses from north to south.

② **Neighboring ecosystems:** forests and meadows.

③ **Maximum altitude:** Kibo Crater, 19,340 feet.

40,000
The number of people visiting Kilimanjaro National Park each year.

Snowy peaks
An aerial view of Kilimanjaro.

A FASCINATING LANDSCAPE

POPULATION
DIFFERENT ETHNIC GROUPS

Daily Life

The Chagga, Masai, and Hadza are just three of the many ethnic groups that live near Mount Kilimanjaro. The Chagga people's livelihood depends on agriculture, and they grow bananas, yams (a type of tuber), beans, and corn. The Masai are a seminomadic tribe that lives in northern Tanzania. They roam the plains raising cattle, sheep, and goats. The Hadza (right) neither raise cattle nor do they grow crops. Instead, they forage the land as their ancestors did 10,000 years ago.

ROUTES OF ASCENT

Mountaineering and Nature

Climbers of Mount Kilimanjaro do not need specific mountaineering experience to climb to the summit successfully, but they do need to be fit and healthy. Most people who climb the mountain do so with the help of a local guide. One of the biggest challenges for climbers is the altitude, which can cause headaches and breathing difficulties. Nearly one-third of climbers fail to reach the summit. There are several routes to the summit, including Rongai, Machame, and Marangu, which is the preferred route.

THE NILE RIVER

The legendary Nile in Egypt is the longest river in Africa and also in the world. (The Amazon River in South America is the largest river by volume of water.) The course of the river's flow of water makes parts of the desert habitable. Also, along the banks of the Nile River emerged one of the most important civilizations: ancient Egypt.

ELEVEN COUNTRIES
TRAVEL

Without Borders

The Nile River runs through 11 countries: Egypt, Sudan, South Sudan, Democratic Republic of Congo, Rwanda, Uganda, Tanzania, Kenya, Ethiopia, Burundi, and Eritrea. It crosses through deserts, forests, savannas, swamps, and mountains. The Nile River Delta is one of the largest deltas in the world, and as a result of its fertile land, it is densely populated.

The Big Meeting

In the city of Khartoum, Sudan's capital, the White Nile from Uganda meets the Blue Nile, which flows from Ethiopia. These two tributaries flow together to form the Nile River.

DESCENT
From its source to its mouth, the Nile drops nearly 6562 feet.

95
The percentage of the Egyptian population that lives in the area of influence of the Nile.

4160 miles
The length of the Nile River.

Satellite Image of the Nile River Its huge delta flows into the Mediterranean.

DAMS
DIKES AND RESERVOIRS

Ecological Damage

Since the late nineteenth century, many dams and reservoirs have been built on the Nile. These dams have caused great ecological damage. An example is the Aswan High Dam, built between 1960 and 1970 in Aswan, Egypt. The dam was seen as a way to ensure a permanent supply of water and a source of hydroelectric power. By damming the Nile, several river species have disappeared and the salt levels of the Delta's water have increased greatly.

Crocodiles

The Nile crocodile is a powerful predator, capable of killing a man.

Monuments

On both sides of the Nile stand great monuments, such as Luxor, the Valley of the Kings, and the Pyramids of Giza.

FLORA AND FAUNA

Africa's rainfall is erratic and many parts of the continent experience regular droughts. Drought, together with humankind's actions, mean that many animal species, such as the gorilla and rhinoceros, are in danger of extinction.

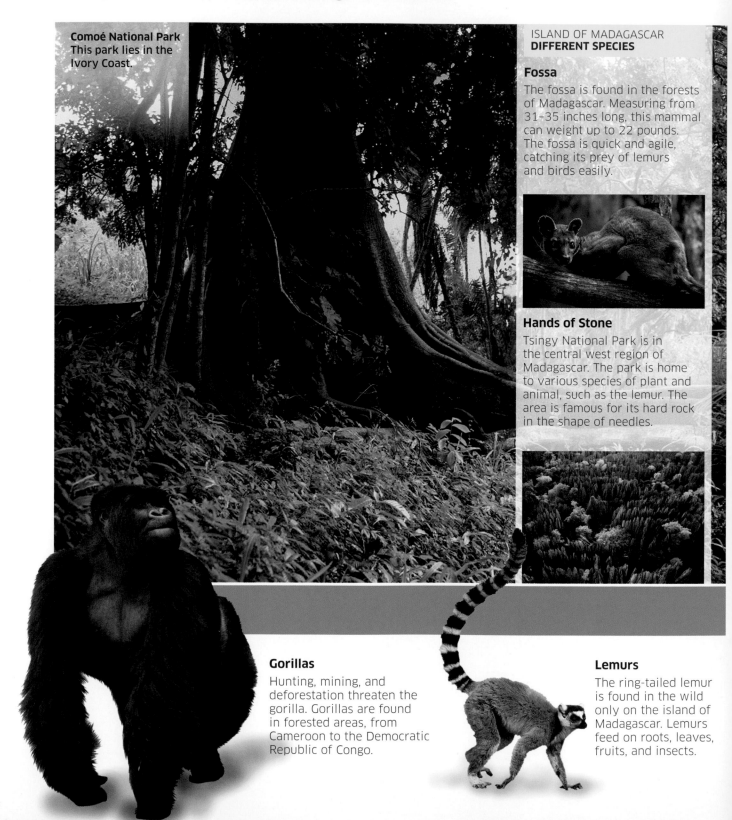

Comoé National Park
This park lies in the Ivory Coast.

ISLAND OF MADAGASCAR
DIFFERENT SPECIES

Fossa
The fossa is found in the forests of Madagascar. Measuring from 31–35 inches long, this mammal can weight up to 22 pounds. The fossa is quick and agile, catching its prey of lemurs and birds easily.

Hands of Stone
Tsingy National Park is in the central west region of Madagascar. The park is home to various species of plant and animal, such as the lemur. The area is famous for its hard rock in the shape of needles.

Gorillas
Hunting, mining, and deforestation threaten the gorilla. Gorillas are found in forested areas, from Cameroon to the Democratic Republic of Congo.

Lemurs
The ring-tailed lemur is found in the wild only on the island of Madagascar. Lemurs feed on roots, leaves, fruits, and insects.

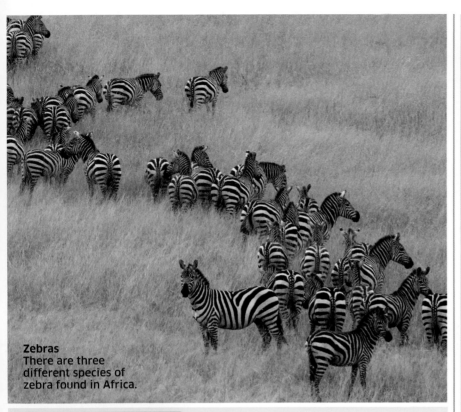

Zebras
There are three
different species of
zebra found in Africa.

DESERT
TYPES OF VEGETATION

Palms

The desert vegetation of Africa has adapted to its environment. While shrubs, grasses, and thorny plants grow in the desert itself, fruit, cereals, and date palms flourish around oases. Date palms are especially useful to the people of the desert. Their leaves are used to provide shade and building materials for furniture, mats, and baskets. The fruit is also eaten.

Baobab

The "upside-down tree" or baobab is found in the semi-arid regions of sub-Saharan Africa. These trees can store up to 264,000 gallons of water. The people of Africa use the tree in many different ways: rope and baskets are made from the bark fiber, and the leaves and fruit are eaten. The fruit is very rich in vitamin C.

RESISTANT MAMMALS

Master of the Desert

Thanks to the camel's strength, these animals are used to carry loads across the desert as well as for farm work. They are also kept for their meat, wool, and skins.

Camels' Feet
A camel won't sink
into sand because it
distributes its weight
on the pads of its feet.

THE OKAVANGO DELTA

This extraordinary natural environment occupies 14.8 million acres and has a rich biodiversity. After the summer rains, the Okavango River in Botswana swells, and the rate of its water flow increases. The river flows to one of the driest areas of the world: the Kalahari Desert.

6487 SQ MI

The surface area of the Okavango Delta.

HIPPO WARNING
Hippopotamuses open their mouths wide to display large fangs. They do this to intimidate their prey.

African jabiru

Hammerhead stork

Hippopotamus

African tiger fish

African pike

BETWEEN WATER AND LAND
The hippopotamus spends the daylight hours semi-submerged in water and the evening out to pasture. Hippos can eat 99 pounds of plants in one night.

PAYBACK
Hippo dung provides nutrients for the aquatic plants. These plants are then fed on by fish, birds, and crocodiles.

APPROPRIATE SUPPORT
The sitatunga antelope has open hooves that are specially adapted for treading on soft ground.

Papyrus

Sitatunga

Wattled crane

Water lily

MARSHLAND
Water from heavy rains in Angola transforms arid land into fertile swamp.

Nile crocodile

ADAPTATIONS
Wetlands are home to a great range of plants and animals. Mammals, reptiles, amphibians, fish, and insects are all found in wetlands. Wetland animals are also adapted to dive into the water. For example, crocodiles have nostrils, eyes, and ears on top of their head, so they can breathe, hear, and see without leaving the water. Hippos can close their nostrils and slow their heart rate down so much that they can stay underwater for half an hour.

GIANT IN THE OKAVANGO

Elephants in the Wild
The Okavango Delta is home to many large herds of elephant. In total, there are about 30,000 elephants in the region.

The animals form herds of females and calves. The presence of elephants is easy to recognize, because they often damage trees, stripping the bark, which is left behind on the ground.

AQUATIC PLANTS
TYPICAL EXAMPLES

Papyrus and Water Sprouts
Plants growing in the wetlands live either entirely or almost entirely submerged in water. **Papyrus**, water lilies, and water sprouts are the most common plants in the habitat. Water birds often walk on the plants in search of food.

Crocodiles
The Nile crocodile is the largest crocodile in Africa. It feeds on fish, antelopes, zebras, buffalo, and poultry.

THE AFRICAN SAVANNA

The African continent has the most extensive savanna in the world. Unlike the North American prairies, the African grasslands have shrubs and trees, such as acacias and baobabs. Many **herbivore** animals live together with their predators in this environment.

Giraffe

African elephant

African marabou

Wildebeest

White-backed vulture

Zebra

Termite

Termite mound

HERBIVORES AND PREDATORS

The savanna is home to many herbivores, grass and plant-eating animals, including buffalo, zebra, wildebeest, elephants, rhinoceros, and giraffe. The predators found in the savanna are lions, leopards, cheetah, and eagles. There are several different species of vulture, which are **scavengers**.

TERMITE SOCIETY

Termites are social insects like bees and ants. The members of each colony build a large nest made from their droppings, which contain sawdust. Inside the mound is a sophisticated network of tunnels to ensure the circulation of fresh air. The tunnels cannot be reached by predators.

ANIMALS
SCAVENGERS

Hyenas

The spotted hyena is found south of the Sahara, from Senegal and the Upper Nile to the southern tip of Africa. The hyena is known for its ungainly body. It scavenges on the prey remains of the big cats, for which it competes with vultures and jackals. In addition, hyenas are highly efficient hunters. To attack their prey, they use their powerful jaws. They also hunt as a pack, allowing them to prey on larger animals, such as zebra, giraffe, and wildebeest.

Data file

Height:	28–35 inches
Weight:	88–154 pounds
Gestation period:	110 days
Number of offspring:	2

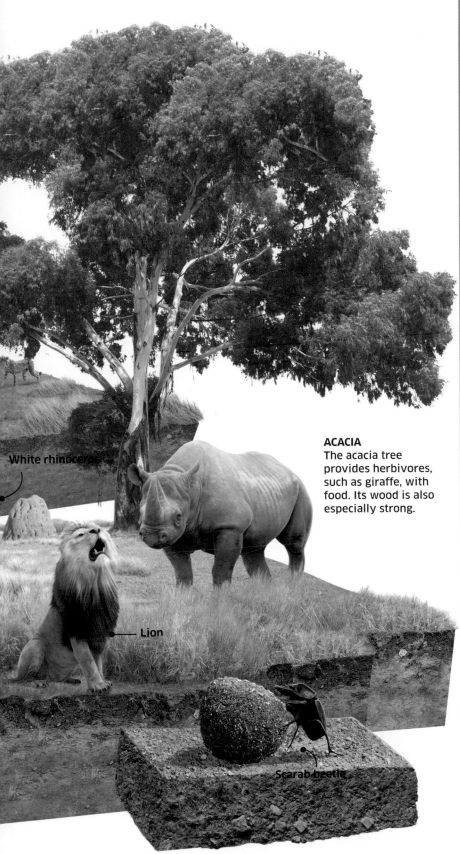

White rhinoceros

ACACIA
The acacia tree provides herbivores, such as giraffe, with food. Its wood is also especially strong.

Lion

Scarab beetle

Vultures

These scavengers are distinguished by their bald heads. By not having feathers on their heads, vultures can sift through the bloody remains of a kill without their heads becoming breeding grounds for parasites and disease. Vultures can have wingspans of up to 8 feet. In addition, they are able to hover in the sky using the air currents in search of prey.

Data file

Height:	37–43 inches
Weight:	up to 18.7 pounds
Gestation period:	55 days
Number of offspring:	1

POPULATION

In Africa, the population is distributed according to each region's natural resources. For example, there are more people in the fertile coastal regions north and west of Nigeria, the Nile Valley, and the eastern plateau. In recent decades, many people in rural areas have migrated to urban cities.

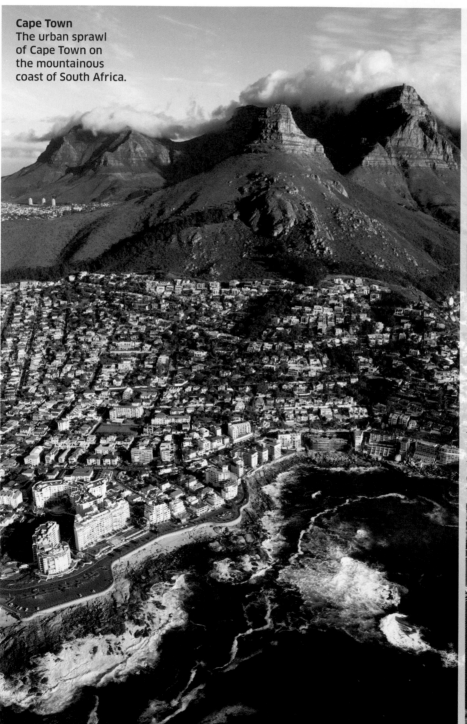

Cape Town
The urban sprawl of Cape Town on the mountainous coast of South Africa.

RAPID GROWTH

Nigerian Children

The rate at which the population grows in Africa is high: the continental average is 2.3 percent each year. Lagos in Nigeria is one of Africa's most populous cities.

Dakar

The site of the current capital of Senegal, Dakar, was first colonized by Europeans in the fifteenth century. The port is in a strategic position for maritime trade with both North America and Europe. Today, it is one of the busiest ports in the world and is used to transport goods, such as chemicals, food, and tobacco, from Mali and Mauritania.

EGYPT
CAIRO

An Important City

Egypt's capital, Cairo, is located on the shores and islands of the Nile River. The city has theaters, universities, and museums. Few places combine the past and present as Cairo does. On the streets of Cairo, it is not uncommon to see carts pulled by donkeys next to expensive modern vehicles. Markets are crowded and the ringing of cell phones and public calls to prayer add to the hubbub of the markets.

REPUBLIC OF SOUTH AFRICA
JOHANNESBURG

Economic and Financial Center

Johannesburg is the largest city in South Africa, one of the continent's wealthiest countries. The wealth stems from the rich gold, diamond, and **platinum** mining industries. Johannesburg's city center is home to 3 million people, but its metropolitan area is home to more than 7 million people. The majority of the population are black South Africans (73 percent).

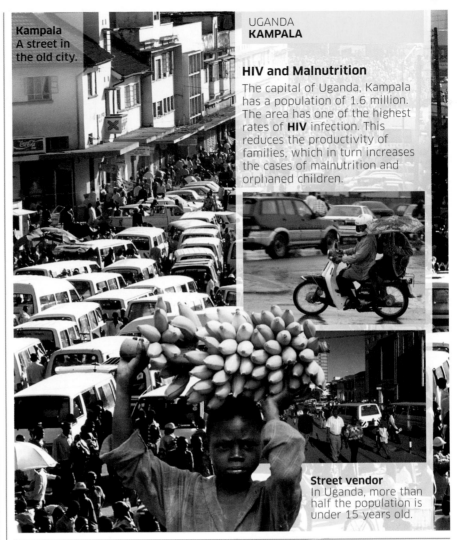

Kampala
A street in the old city.

UGANDA
KAMPALA

HIV and Malnutrition

The capital of Uganda, Kampala has a population of 1.6 million. The area has one of the highest rates of **HIV** infection. This reduces the productivity of families, which in turn increases the cases of malnutrition and orphaned children.

Street vendor
In Uganda, more than half the population is under 15 years old.

MOROCCO
MARRAKECH

Trade Center

The city of Marrakech was founded in 1062 by the Arabs. It became an important trading center with the rest of Africa. Marrakech was a point of arrival and departure for merchants, and the city's wealth attracted builders and craftspeople. Today, the city is known for its market, which offers a variety of goods, from traditional crafts to modern appliances.

PEOPLE AND LANGUAGES

With more than 3000 different groups of peoples in Africa, many have retained their identity by keeping their own language. Today, there are more than 2000 different languages spoken in Africa. The continent also has English, French, and Arabic-speaking countries as a result of colonial times.

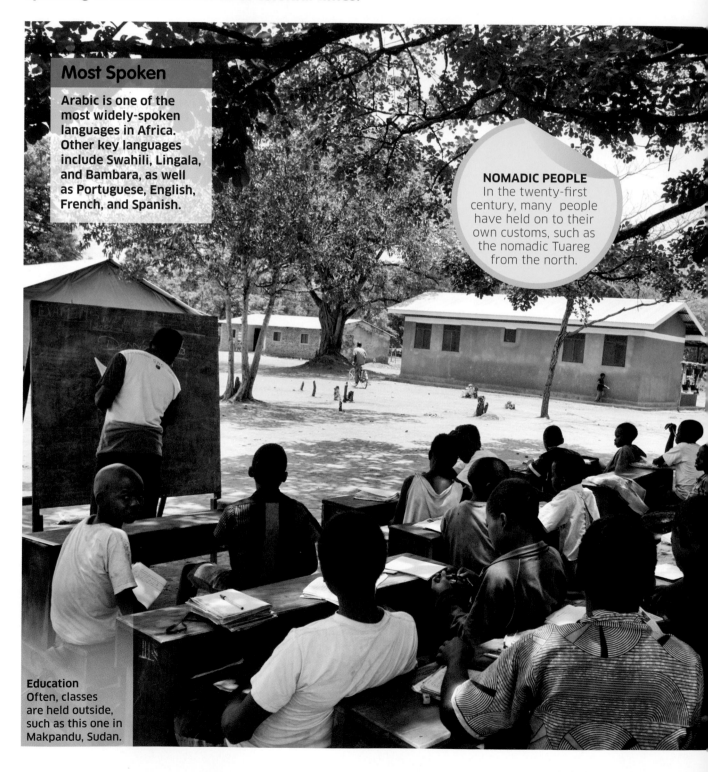

Most Spoken

Arabic is one of the most widely-spoken languages in Africa. Other key languages include Swahili, Lingala, and Bambara, as well as Portuguese, English, French, and Spanish.

NOMADIC PEOPLE
In the twenty-first century, many people have held on to their own customs, such as the nomadic Tuareg from the north.

Education
Often, classes are held outside, such as this one in Makpandu, Sudan.

Papyrus

The papyrus plant that grows in the Nile Valley was used by ancient Egyptians to make paper. This invention means we now know about written history.

Muslims

After their conquests of the seventh century, the Arabs brought Islam to the territories of North Africa.

CULTURAL ISSUES
DIFFERENT HISTORIES

Four Groups

Experts have divided the many African languages into four main families:

1. Afro-Asian (Arabic, Berber)
2. Niger-Congo (Bantu, Zulu)
3. Nilo-Saharan (Fur, Songhai)
4. Khoisan (Khoi, San)

Religions

There is a great variety of religions on the continent. Often, a religion blends two or more of these. For example:

1. **Animism**
2. **Polytheism**
3. **Islam**
4. **Christianity**

Great Kingdoms

Many different civilizations formed powerful kingdoms that flourished on the continent. For example:

1. **Egypt (3000–332 BC)**
2. **Ghana (800–1235)**
3. **Mali (1200–1600)**
4. **Benin (1500–1600)**
5. **Northern Arab Caliphates (641–1171)**

European Colonization

From 1884 to 1885, the European powers divided most of the continent into colonies. Although Spain, Germany, and Belgium had their own colonies, most countries were colonized by:

1. **France**
2. **Great Britain**
3. **Portugal**

VARIETY
AFRICAN TRIBES

CAMEROON–CONGO–ANGOLA
BANTU

Villagers

A variety of peoples who speak Bantu languages have held on to their traditional customs and base their economy on agriculture.

CONGO
PYGMIES

Gatherers

Large populations of pygmy, or very small, people are found in the forested areas of the Congo. These people are gatherers.

KENYA–TANZANIA
MASAI

Semi-Nomadic People

The life of the Masai revolves around raising cattle, sheep and goats. There are around 900,000 Masai on the continent.

DESERTS
BEDOUIN

Nomadic Herders

The Bedouins of North Africa are Muslim and speak several dialects of Arabic.

THE SAN PEOPLE

The San, or Bushmen, are the native people of southern Africa. Originally, they were found in South Africa, Zimbabwe, Lesotho, Mozambique, Swaziland, Botswana, Namibia, and Angola. These people were traditionally hunter-gatherers, and today, their dwindling tribe is found mainly in the Kalahari Desert.

OUR PAST
WHAT MODERN SCIENCE TELLS US

Africa: Starting Point

According to modern genetic studies, the San are the oldest living tribe. It is believed that they are one of the original tribes from whom all others evolved. The San are typically short people with light skin and curly hair. A typical member of the San tribe has a thick layer of skin over the eyes, called the epicanthic fold, which is also characteristic of the peoples of the East.

USING SOUND TO COMMUNICATE

Peculiarity

The language spoken by the San is characterized by its clicking or popping sounds, a feature found in the languages of other groups of ancient African tribes.

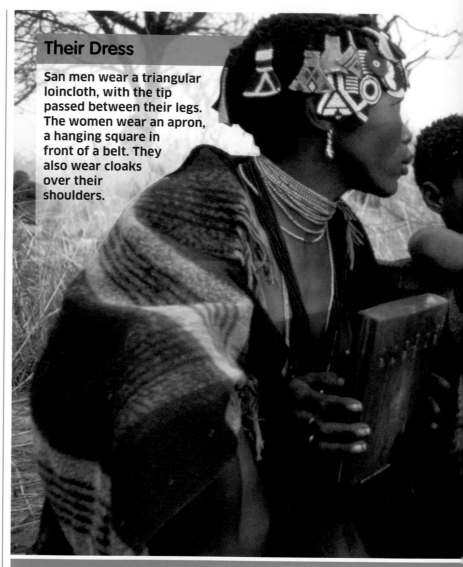

Their Dress

San men wear a triangular loincloth, with the tip passed between their legs. The women wear an apron, a hanging square in front of a belt. They also wear cloaks over their shoulders.

Kalahari Desert

The San are found in the dry Kalahari Desert. They obtain food by hunting animals and gathering plants. Some San have found work as shepherds.

Water Collection

To survive, the San have to be able to find water. They suck water from plant roots and empty ostrich eggs. This image (left) shows an ostrich egg next to a hen's egg.

Hunters

San men hunt alone or with their children, using bows and arrows. Their arrows are dipped in poison, which they get from poisonous snakes.

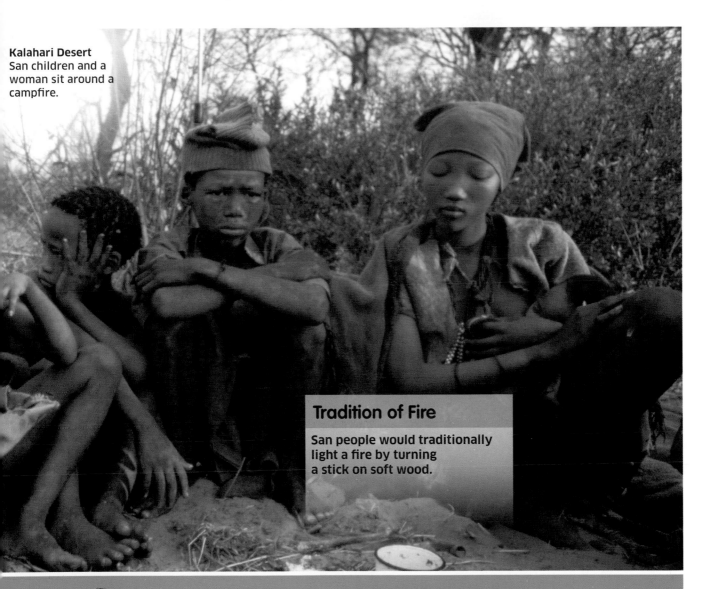

Kalahari Desert
San children and a woman sit around a campfire.

Tradition of Fire

San people would traditionally light a fire by turning a stick on soft wood.

Houses

San shelters are made by the women wherever there is vegetation. When their food supply runs out, the group will move to another area.

Art

San cave paintings are some of the oldest in the world. Their paintings often tell a hunting story. This example (left) is found in a cave in Murewa, Zimbabwe.

ECONOMIC RESOURCES

Africa may often appear to lack wealth. However, its natural resources offer huge potential wealth. The continent has the greatest sources of precious stones and metals in the world. South Africa has some of the richest companies and industries on the continent.

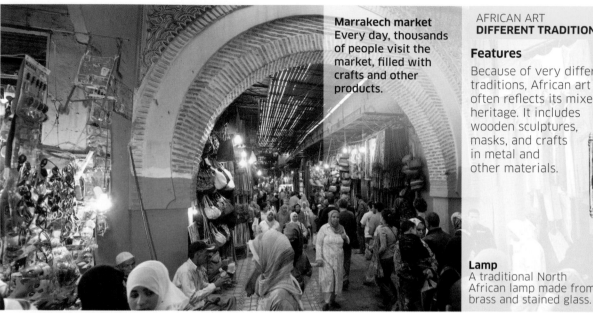

Marrakech market
Every day, thousands of people visit the market, filled with crafts and other products.

AFRICAN ART
DIFFERENT TRADITIONS

Features

Because of very different traditions, African art often reflects its mixed heritage. It includes wooden sculptures, masks, and crafts in metal and other materials.

Lamp
A traditional North African lamp made from brass and stained glass.

KENYA
FARMING

Subsistence and Export

There are two types of farming on the African continent. The first is called subsistence farming. Here, a farmer will work small areas of land, growing just enough food for the farmer and the immediate family. The second type of farming is large-scale agriculture for the export of crops. This type of farming now occupies nearly 40 percent of land that is suitable for farming. It consists of large plantations, often owned by foreign companies. The most common crops grown include cocoa, bananas, coffee, and tea.

TOURISM
SAFARIS

Most Visited

Tourism provides a great source of income for the continent. Many visitors go on safari in Kenya and Tanzania to see African wildlife in its natural habitat.

A tea picker in Kenya.

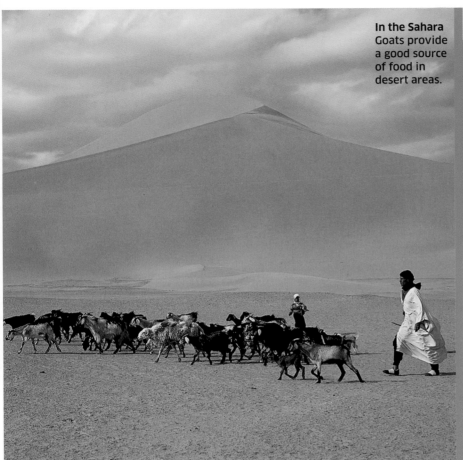

In the Sahara Goats provide a good source of food in desert areas.

Consuming Local Food

Africa has rich resources of fish. A good source of food, most fish caught is eaten locally. Only Morocco, Senegal, Ivory Coast, South Africa, and Namibia are countries rich enough to be able to export their fish. The Great Lakes region has many amazing freshwater fish, too. Countries such as Tanzania, Uganda, Kenya, and Nigeria catch these freshwater fish.

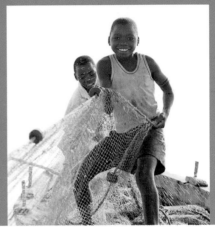

Timber Production

In recent years, African forests have been in danger from people who have begun to cut down a large number of trees. Areas of forest that are near sea ports or larger local markets have lost the greatest numbers of trees.

In the Central African Republic, for example, between 15 and 18 different types of tree are being cut down, while in the Democratic Republic of Congo, 18 to 20 species are disappearing. Many environmental groups fear that these actions will destroy the habitats of many species of animal, especially the gorilla, whose numbers are dwindling.

A lumberjack cutting a tree with a chainsaw.

Peasant Women

Around 70 percent of farm work in the region is done by women. However, most of the income from agriculture is controlled by men. This tradition has led to great inequalities between men and women in their households.

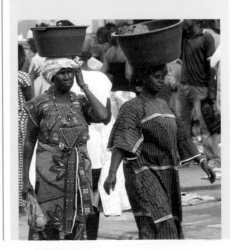

CAIRO

Located on the Nile River, Cairo is the largest city in the Arab world and Africa. Rich in ancient monuments, theaters, and museums, this historic center was declared a World Heritage Site by UNESCO.

Country	Egypt
Area	175 sq mi
Population	7,010,000
Density	40,080 people/sq mi

CITY EMBLEMS

The Alabaster Mosque

Built between 1830 and 1848, this mosque consists of a central dome surrounded by four others, and has two equal minarets that stand 269 feet tall. Below, you can see the front and inside of the building.

The Cairo Tower
Located in the Zamalek district, this television tower is 617 feet tall. On the fourteenth floor there is a revolving restaurant.

Mosque of Al-Azhar

This mosque was built almost 1040 years ago. Its name means "the most splendid."

Madrasa al-Taybarsiyya
Originally designed to complement the mosque of Al-Azhar, the Madrasa al-Taybarsiyya was built in 1309. It houses the tomb of Prince Amir Taybars.

Mosque of Al-Azhar
The mosque is in the center of the city.

Street Fairs

The souk, or market, of Cairo is a maze of narrow streets and tiny shops filled with goods of all kinds, such as slippers, scarves, glass pipes, spices, or jewelry.

The Egyptian Museum

This museum holds the greatest collection of objects from ancient Egypt, and has more than 120,000 pieces. Over 2.5 million people visit the museum every year.

Minaret Qaitbay
Built in 1483, this cylindrical tower has three balconies and arched panels. It was from these towers that the call to prayer came.

Egyptian Pastries
Egyptian bakeries are famous for their delicate pastries, which are made of almonds, honey, cereals, and grits.

A THOUSAND MINARETS
Cairo is known as the city of "the thousand minarets," which refers to the number of mosques in the city.

Religion
The majority of the city's population are Muslim. These girls are wearing traditional Muslim veils.

Demography
The inhabitants are mostly descendants of the ancient Egyptians, Arabs, Bedouins, and Berbers.

THE PYRAMIDS OF GIZA

Opposite the city of Cairo, across the Nile River, the mighty pyramids of Giza rise majestically. Built 4500 years ago, the pyramids house the tombs of the **pharaohs** Khufu, Khafre, and Menkaure. They are the greatest symbol of the culture of ancient Egypt.

MAP OF THE VALLEY OF THE KINGS

Location

The valley is home to the three most famous Egyptian pyramids: Khufu, Khufu's son, Khafre, and Menkaure. The map below shows how the complex was laid out.

1 Pyramid of Khufu
2 Pyramid of Khafre
3 Pyramid of Menkaure
4 Great Sphinx
5 Great Temple
6 Procession route
7 Tomb of a dignitary
8 Mortuary temple
9 Secondary pyramid

The Great Sphinx
Carved from a single rock, it has the body of a lion and a human face.

3,297,343 cubic yds

The total volume of the pyramid of Khufu.

Gold peak

The white limestone at the top was covered with a shiny metal, possibly gold.

Khufu

Two million stones, each weighing 440 pounds, were used to build this pyramid. The pyramid is the same height as a 40-story building.

Small pyramids

East of the pyramid of Khufu, three other smaller pyramids were found.

Possible ramp methods

Multiple	Perimeter	Step	Front only

Ramp System

No one is sure quite how the pyramids were built, but it is known that large blocks of stone were loaded using a complex system of ramps.

Khafre

The pyramid of Khafre is guarded by the Great Sphinx, a symbol of the pharaoh.

Destination

The pyramids were built to protect the dead pharoah's body. Khufu's pyramid took 33 years to build.

VILLAGE
Near the Sphinx, there was a town where officials and the workers responsible for the construction of the pyramids lived.

Menkaure

In Menkaure's burial chamber, an empty sarcophagus (stone coffin) was found.

Spectacular sight
The pyramids
at sunset.

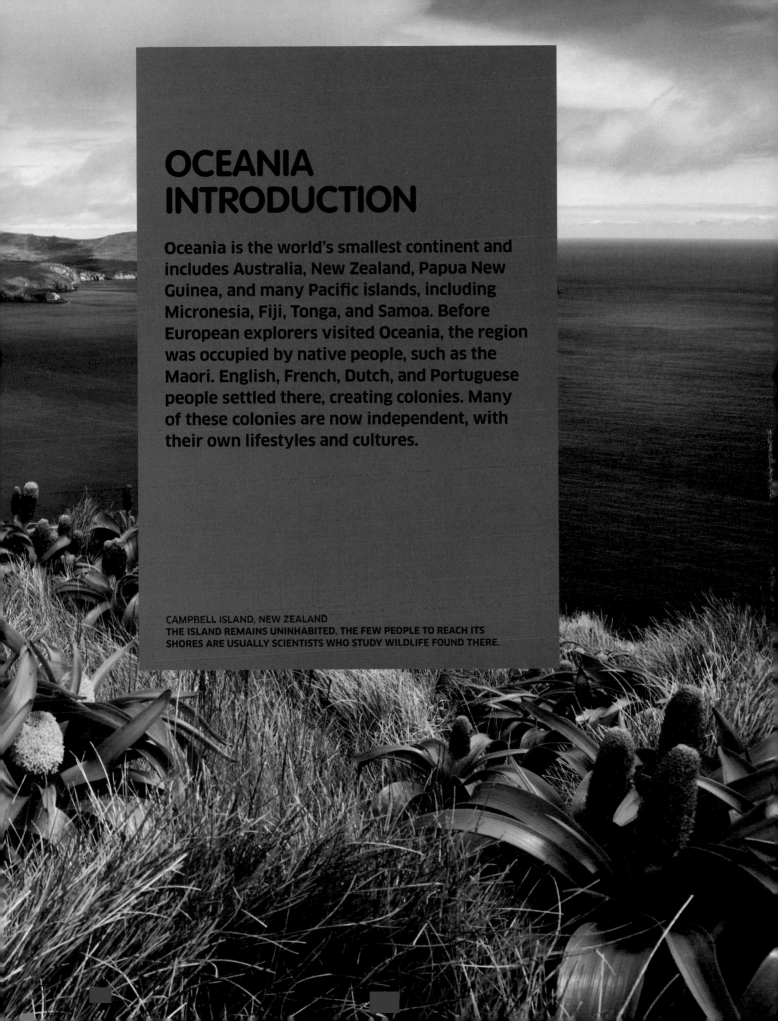

OCEANIA INTRODUCTION

Oceania is the world's smallest continent and includes Australia, New Zealand, Papua New Guinea, and many Pacific islands, including Micronesia, Fiji, Tonga, and Samoa. Before European explorers visited Oceania, the region was occupied by native people, such as the Maori. English, French, Dutch, and Portuguese people settled there, creating colonies. Many of these colonies are now independent, with their own lifestyles and cultures.

CAMPBELL ISLAND, NEW ZEALAND
THE ISLAND REMAINS UNINHABITED. THE FEW PEOPLE TO REACH ITS
SHORES ARE USUALLY SCIENTISTS WHO STUDY WILDLIFE FOUND THERE.

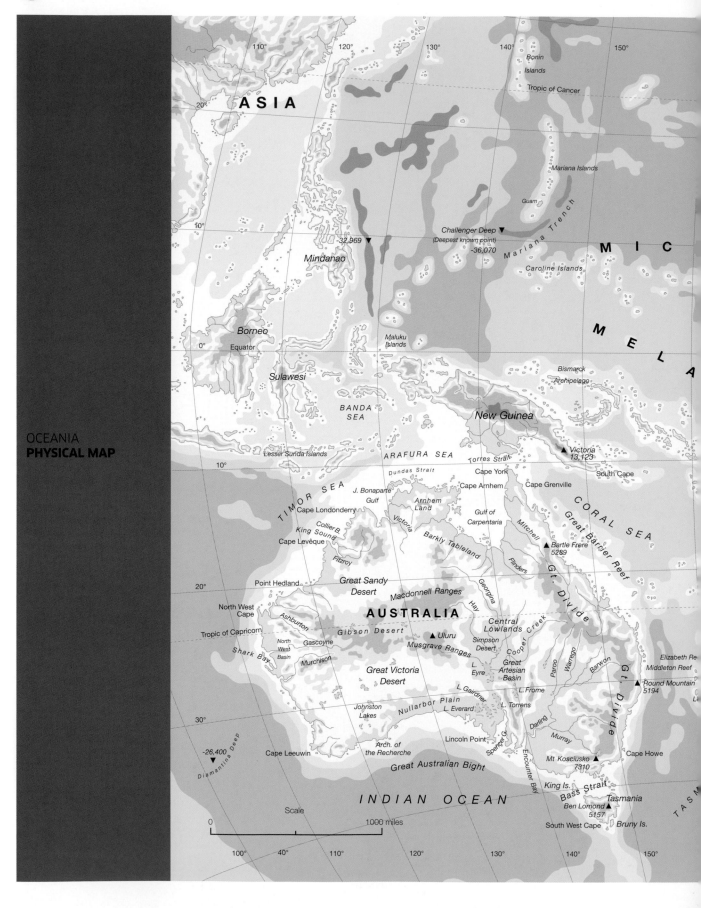

OCEANIA
PHYSICAL MAP

ASIA

110° 120° 130° 140° 150°

Bonin
Islands

Tropic of Cancer

20°

Mariana Islands

10°

Guam

M I C

Challenger Deep ▼
-32,969 ▼   (Deepest known point)
-36,070

Mariana Trench

Mindanao

Caroline Islands

M E L A

Borneo
0°   Equator

Bismarck
Archipelago

Sulawesi

Maluku
Islands

BANDA
SEA

New Guinea

▲ Victoria
13,123

Lesser Sunda Islands

ARAFURA SEA

Torres Strait

Dundas Strait

Cape York

South Cape

10°

Cape Arnhem

Cape Grenville

T I M O R   S E A

J. Bonaparte
Gulf

Cape Londonderry

Arnhem
Land

Gulf of
Carpentaria

CORAL SEA

Collier B.

Victoria

King Sound

Cape Levêque

Fitzroy

Barkly Tableland

Mitchell

Great Barrier Reef

▲ Bartle Frere
5289

Flinders

Point Hedland

Great Sandy
Desert

Macdonnell Ranges

Georgina

Gt. Divide

20°

North West
Cape

AUSTRALIA

Hay

Central
Lowlands

Ashburton

Cooper Creek

Elizabeth Re
Middleton Reef

Tropic of Capricorn

North
West
Basin

Gascoyne

Gibson Desert

▲ Uluru

Simpson
Desert

Paroo

Warrego

Barwon

Gt. Divide

Shark Bay

Murchison

Musgrave Ranges

Great
Artesian
Basin

▲ Round Mountain
5194

Great Victoria
Desert

L.
Eyre

L. Frome

Johnston
Lakes

Nullarbor Plain

L Gardner

L. Everard

L. Torrens

Darling

Murray

30°

Cape Leeuwin

Arch. of
the Recherche

Lincoln Point

Spencer G.

Encounter Bay

Cape Howe

-26,400 ▼

Diamantina Deep

Great Australian Bight

Mt Kosciusko
7310 ▲

King Is.

Bass Strait

Tasmania

TASM

I N D I A N   O C E A N

Ben Lomond ▲
5157

Scale

South West Cape

Bruny Is.

0   1000 miles

100°   40°   110°   120°   130°   140°   150°

170° 180° 170° 160° 150° 140° 130° 120°

Hawaii Ridge

P O L Y N E S I A

Hawaiian Islands

Necker — Nihoa

Kaua'i
O'ahu
Maui
Mauna Kea ▲ Hawaii
13,796 ▲ Mauna Loa
13,678

20°

N O R T H   P A C I F I C   O C E A N

10°

Marshall Trench

Ratak Chain

M I C R O N E S I A

E S I A

Fanning Ridge

Teraina
Tabuaeran
Kiritimati

0°

Gilbert Islands

Jarvis Is.

Tuvalu Islands

Phoenix Islands

Malden Is.
Starbuck Is.

Cruz Is.

Tokelau

Caroline Is.

Marquesas Islands

10°

Manihiki

Wallis Is.

Samoan Islands

Suwarrow

A

Futuna Is.

Vanuatu Archipelago

Leeward Islands
Tahiti

Tuamotu Archipelago

Fiji Islands

Lau Islands

Tonga Islands

Cook Islands

Windward Islands

Archipelago de la Société

Niue

Loyalty Islands

Hunter Islands

Rarotonga

20°

-35,702 ▼

Tubuai Islands

Gambier Islands

Henderson Is.

Norfolk Is.

Keramadec-Tonga Trench

Keramadec Islands
Raoul Is.
Curtis Is.

-31,079 ▼

Rapa Iti
Bass Islands

Pitcairn Islands

120°

▼
-32,963

ree Kings Is. *North Cape*

S O U T H   P A C I F I C   O C E A N

30°

North Island
Bay of Plenty
East Cape
Mt. Taranaki
8264 ▲
L. Taupo
Hawke Bay

South Pacific Basin

NEW
LAND

Cook
2,349 ▲

Tapuae-o-Uenuku
9465 ▲

Chatham Islands

South Island

L. Te Anau

170° 180° 170° 160° 150° 140° 130° 40° 120° 110°

Bounty Is.

KEY		
Altitude (in feet)		
		13,000 or over
		6500
		1600
		650
		0
		-650 (depression)
Depth (in feet)		
		0
		-650
		-6500
		-13,000
		-19,500

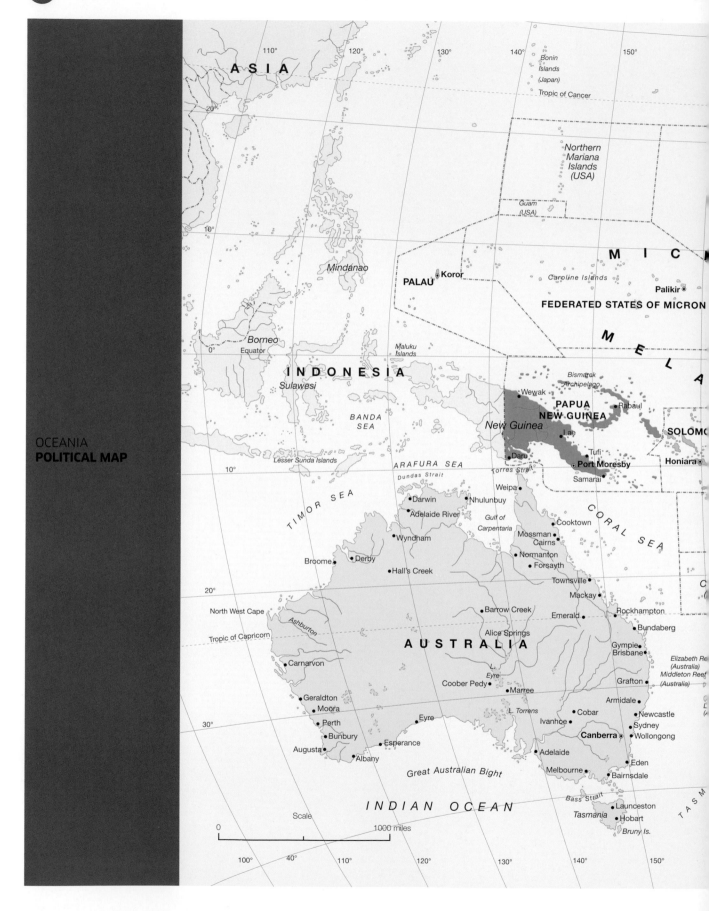

OCEANIA
POLITICAL MAP

ASIA

110° 120° 130° 140° Bonin 150°
Islands
(Japan)

Tropic of Cancer

20°

Northern
Mariana
Islands
(USA)

10°

Guam
(USA)

M I C

Mindanao

PALAU Koror Caroline Islands Palikir

FEDERATED STATES OF MICRON

M E L A

Borneo

0° Equator

Maluku
Islands

INDONESIA

Bismarck
Archipelago

Wewak Rabaul

Sulawesi

BANDA
SEA

PAPUA
NEW GUINEA

New Guinea Lae

SOLOMO

Lesser Sunda Islands

ARAFURA SEA

Torres Strait

Dundas Strait

Tufi

Daru Port Moresby Honiara

Samarai

10°

Weipa

CORAL SEA

Darwin Nhulunbuy

Adelaide River Gulf of Cooktown
Carpentaria

Wyndham Mossman
Cairns

Broome Derby Normanton

Hall's Creek Forsayth

Townsville

Mackay

20°

Barrow Creek Emerald Rockhampton

North West Cape Ashburton Bundaberg

Tropic of Capricorn Alice Springs

AUSTRALIA Gympie
Brisbane

Carnarvon Elizabeth Re
(Australia)

Eyre Middleton Reef
Coober Pedy (Australia)

Geraldton Marree Grafton

Moora Armidale

30° Perth Eyre L. Torrens Cobar Newcastle

Bunbury Ivanhoe Sydney

Augusta Esperance Canberra Wollongong

Albany Adelaide

Great Australian Bight Eden

Melbourne Bairnsdale

Bass Strait TASM

INDIAN OCEAN Launceston

Scale Tasmania Hobart

0 1000 miles Bruny Is.

100° 40° 110° 120° 130° 140° 150°

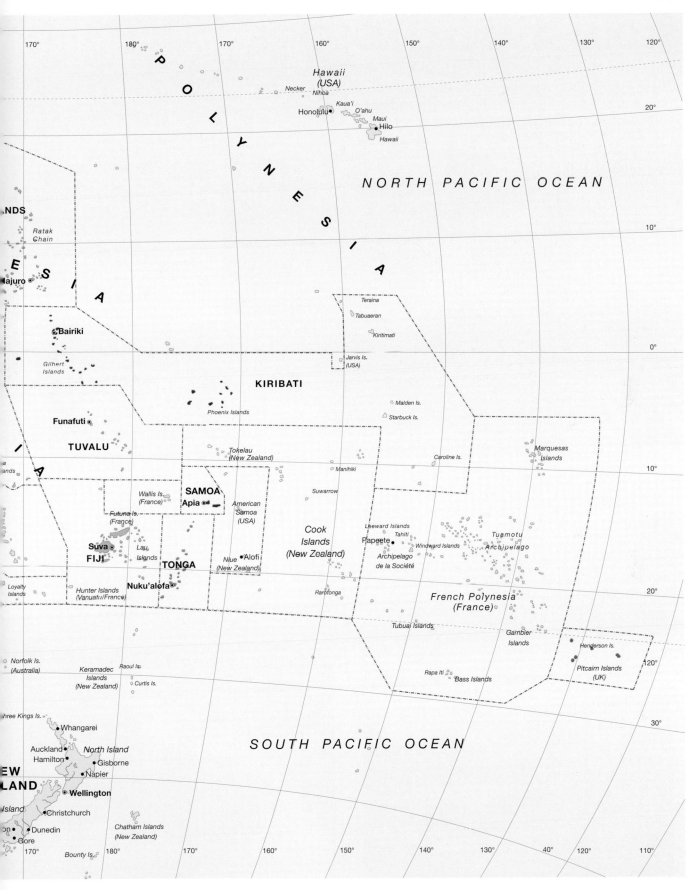

170° 180° 170° 160° 150° 140° 130° 120°

P
O
L
Y
N
E
S
I
A

*Hawaii
(USA)*

Necker
Nihoa
Kaua'i
O'ahu
Honolulu●
Maui
●Hilo
Hawaii

20°

NORTH PACIFIC OCEAN

10°

NDS

*Ratak
Chain*

●ajuro

E

A

A

Teraina

Tabuaeran

Kiritimati

0°

●**Bairiki**

*Gilbert
Islands*

Jarvis Is.
(USA)

KIRIBATI

Malden Is.

Starbuck Is.

Phoenix Islands

*Marquesas
Islands*

●**Funafuti**

TUVALU

*Tokelau
(New Zealand)*

Manihiki

Caroline Is.

10°

I
A

A

ands

*Wallis Is.
(France)*

SAMOA
Apia●■

Suwarrow

*Futuna Is.
(France)*

*American
Samoa
(USA)*

Leeward Islands

Tahiti

*Tuamotu
Archipelago*

●**Suva**

*Lau
Islands*

FIJI

Niue ●Alofi

*Cook
Islands
(New Zealand)*

Papeete●

Windward Islands

TONGA

(New Zealand)

*Archipelago
de la Société*

*Loyalty
Islands*

*Hunter Islands
(Vanuatu/France)*

Nuku'alofa●

Rarotonga

*French Polynesia
(France)*

20°

Tubuai Islands

*Gambier
Islands*

Henderson Is.

120°

○ *Norfolk Is.
(Australia)*

*Keramadec
Islands
(New Zealand)*

Raoul Is.

Curtis Is.

Rapa Iti

Bass Islands

*Pitcairn Islands
(UK)*

30°

hree Kings Is.

●Whangarei

SOUTH PACIFIC OCEAN

Auckland●
Hamilton●

North Island
●Gisborne

EW

●Napier

●**Wellington**

LAND

Island

●Christchurch

*Chatham Islands
(New Zealand)*

on ●
● Dunedin
● Gore

170° 180° 170° 160° 150° 140° 130° 40° 120° 110°

Bounty Is.

GEOLOGY AND LANDSCAPE

Originally, Oceania and Antarctica were one landmass called Gondwana. As a result of continental drift, lands split apart into the many volcanic islands and coral reefs that are found in the Pacific Ocean today.

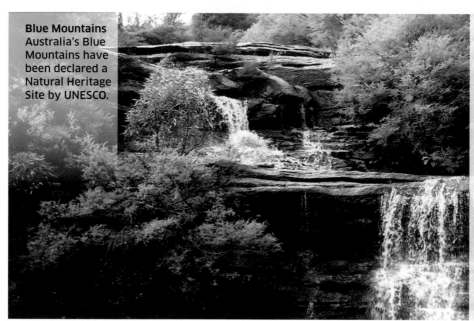

Blue Mountains
Australia's Blue Mountains have been declared a Natural Heritage Site by UNESCO.

MOUNTAINS AND SNOW
AUSTRALIA

Three Sisters

These rock formations are found in the Blue Mountains in the Australian state of New South Wales. Each "sister" is just over 2953 feet high. They were formed when the sandstone eroded.

NATIONAL PARKS
NEW ZEALAND

Tongariro and Its Holy Sites

Tongariro on the North Island is New Zealand's oldest national park. It holds a great spiritual importance for the original inhabitants of New Zealand, the Maori. The park has three active volcanoes, which add to its natural beauty. Visitors to the park can walk along the many trails, and for the more adventurous, there is whitewater rafting.

NATURAL RESOURCES
TOURISM IN PROTECTED AREAS

Arthur's Pass, New Zealand

Arthur's Pass is the highest pass over New Zealand's Southern Alps. It is named after Arthur Dudley Dobson, who found his way over the pass in 1864, but the route was already known to the Maori. The highest peak in the Southern Alps is the 7874-foot-high Mount Murchison. Popular activities include rock climbing, mountain biking, and hiking.

GEOGRAPHY AND CLIMATE
THE WORLD'S SMALLEST CONTINENT

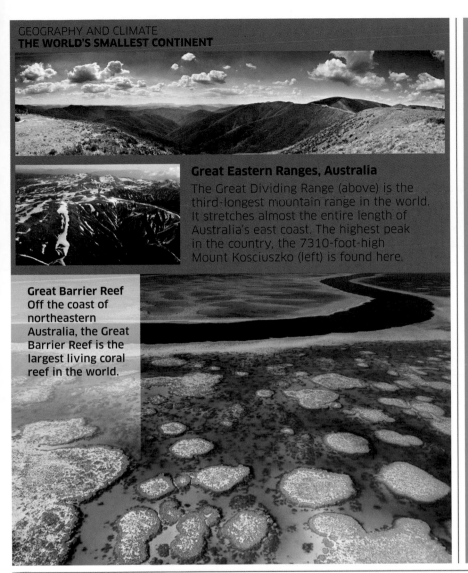

Great Eastern Ranges, Australia

The Great Dividing Range (above) is the third-longest mountain range in the world. It stretches almost the entire length of Australia's east coast. The highest peak in the country, the 7310-foot-high Mount Kosciuszko (left) is found here.

Great Barrier Reef

Off the coast of northeastern Australia, the Great Barrier Reef is the largest living coral reef in the world.

SEAS AND VOLCANOES
POLLUTION WATCH

Timor Sea

Located between the island of Timor and Australia, the Timor Sea borders the Indian Ocean. In 2009, there was a major oil spill there, which had a disastrous effect on birds, marine invertebrates, coral, and algae.

Mount Egmont, New Zealand

Called Taranaki by the Maori, Mount Egmont is a dormant volcano, 8261 feet high. The volcano was last active in 1655. Other active volcanoes on the North Island include Ruapehu, Ngauruhoe, and Tongariro.

Uluru

Found in central Australia, this red sandstone rock is sacred to the Aboriginal people of the area.

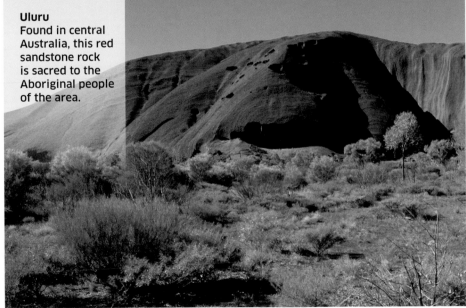

AUSTRALIA
ULURU

Sacred Rock

Located in Australia's Northern Territory, Uluru is just one of the attractions of the Uluru-Kata Tjuta National Park. This giant red rock stands 1142 feet high. Considered one of the most important sites in Aboriginal culture, the rock is frequently visited by Aboriginals for ceremonies and rituals.

FLORA AND FAUNA

Some exotic plants and animals came to Oceania with the arrival of foreign explorers and settlers. However, Australia still has many species that are found nowhere else, including the kangaroo, the Tasmanian devil, and the koala bear.

Lupins
These striking plants were brought to New Zealand by settlers from Europe.

PROTECTED SPECIES
LIVING FOSSILS

Reptile

The tuatara lizard is found in New Zealand. Its name means "spiny back" in Maori. It grows to 27.5 inches long and is considered a living fossil because it is not found anywhere else on the planet.

EXOTIC SPECIES
NOW A PEST

Mynah Bird

The mynah bird is native to Asia. It was introduced to the region by the British to control crop pests. Today, this bird is considered to be a pest in both rural and urban areas and is a threat to the native bird species of Oceania.

MOVIE MAGIC
FINDING NEMO

Clownfish

The clownfish lives in the Pacific Ocean. Easily recognized by their bright orange color, clownfish are carnivorous and live with sea anemones on the coral reefs of the Pacific.

Frigate Bird

The frigate bird is a symbol on the flag of the island nation of Kiribati. It is easily identified by its swollen red throat.

BIRD OF PARADISE
The bird of paradise is the national bird of Papua New Guinea.

Brown Booby

The brown booby bird is found along the coastlines of Tuvalu, Micronesia, French Polynesia, and Australia. Brown boobies eat mainly small fish or squid that gather in groups near the surface of the ocean.

Surgeonfish

Diversity

There are 1500 species of fish and 2200 plant species living on the Great Barrier Reef.

Angelfish

Butterflyfish

Tasmanian Devil

The Tasmanian devil is an aggressive carnivorous **marsupial**. It is found only on the island of Tasmania, off the coast of southern Australia.

Koala

This plant-eating marsupial grows up to 29.5 inches long.

Saltwater crocodile
The saltwater crocodile is the largest and most dangerous crocodile in the world.

Kiwi

The kiwi bird is the official symbol of New Zealand. The kiwi is a very rare bird that is active mainly at night. Kiwi birds cannot fly because their wings are too small.

Eucalyptus
The eucalyptus is the most common native tree in Australia.

POPULATION AND ECONOMY

Australia and New Zealand are the largest countries in Oceania, but they have some of the lowest population densities. These two countries have developed and stable economies with strong trade links to Southeast Asia. Many of the smaller countries and colonies in Oceania struggle to get by on income from tourism and agriculture.

Sydney, Australia
Pedestrians cross between George Street and Park Avenue, in the heart of the city.

NEW ZEALAND
CITIES

Auckland
The largest city in New Zealand, Auckland has two ports. It is also the economic and cultural center of the country.

Government
In 1893, New Zealand became the first country in the world to recognize the right of women to vote. While some colonies are fighting for independence, most countries in the region are democracies.

Boat Taxis
These are used by the people of Micronesia to get around. They are also rented out to tourists visiting the islands.

Australian Industry
Australia is the most advanced country in the region. It has large chemical, petrochemical, food, and beverage industries.

New Zealand
This country is one of the largest sheep farming nations in the world.

CONTRASTING INFRASTRUCTURE

Houghton Highway

The longest bridge in Oceania is the Houghton Highway in Queensland, Australia. This **viaduct** is 8990 feet long. While Australia has 505,157 miles of road, Tuvalu has just 5 miles. Most countries in the region trade by sea.

Wine industry
Australia is a large producer of wine. It is the fourth-largest exporter of wine in the world.

City link
The Sydney monorail runs through the city.

RICHNESS OF PEOPLE AND LANGUAGES

Micronesia

This is a group of thousands of small islands in the western Pacific Ocean. Many of the islands are now small independent nations. Micronesia has a wide variety of cultures, and its people speak many different languages. The people are descended from settlers who came from other parts of the Pacific.

MINING
A GREAT RESOURCE

Australia's Mining Industry

Australia is the second-largest gold producer in the world and the leading producer of **bauxite**, **titanium**, and diamonds. The country also mines **uranium**, nickel, lead, zinc, tin, and copper, and has its own oil fields. These natural resources are very important to the country's economy.

ABORIGINAL AUSTRALIANS

Aboriginal Australians were the first people to settle in Australia. Traditionally, they lived as hunter-gatherers, hunting and foraging food from the land. There are many different Aboriginal groups across the continent, each with its own language and traditions.

COMMON HERITAGE

Out of Africa

About 80,000 years ago, a small group of people left Africa and crossed into Arabia in search of food. All non-Africans, from Europeans to Amerindians to Aboriginal Australians, are descended from this group. Some of the people who left Africa at this time moved along the southern coast of Asia, reaching Australia about 50,000 years ago. These were the ancestors of today's Aboriginal Australian people.

CULTURE AND TRADITIONS

Body Painting

Body decoration using ancestral designs is an important part of many ceremonies. Designs are painted onto the face and body using ochers (natural clays) that are ground and mixed with water.

Aboriginal culture
Boys perform a traditional dance.

Dance

Dance is an important part of Aboriginal culture. Dancing may be part of a social gathering or to mark a specific occasion, such as the opening of a new building.

Cave Art

These rock paintings in Kakadu National Park represent scenes from a mythical world. The paintings are many thousands of years old.

Didgeridoo
This wind instrument is used in dance and music. A didgeridoo may be 2.5–6.5 feet long. The larger the instrument, the deeper its sound.

Stone Mortar
A stone mortar was traditionally used to grind or crush herbs and seeds used for cooking.

Men and women

Male dancing is lively with a lot of jumping and kicking. Women have their own dances, which are less energetic and more of a loose-knee shuffle.

Homes
In the past, Aboriginal people did not build houses or huts but lived in caves. Today, many Aborigines still live in the Australian **outback**, but in houses.

Boomerang
This flat, wooden weapon was traditionally used for hunting. The boomerang was thrown at its target. If it missed, the boomerang would spin around and return to the person who had thrown it.

THE SYDNEY OPERA HOUSE

One of the world's most recognizable buildings, the Sydney Opera House contains a large hall for opera, a concert hall, large and small theaters, an exhibition area, and a library.

BUILDING DETAILS

A Palace of Culture

The Sydney Opera House was declared a World Heritage Site by UNESCO in 2007.

Fact File

Location:
Sydney, Australia

Kind of building:
Cultural center

Capacity (of performing spaces):
5700 spectators

Structure:
Cement, pink granite, and wood veneer

1 Opera house
2 Concert hall
3 Restaurant

City postcard
The Sydney Opera House was opened in 1973. It cost AU$102 million to build.

Utzon Hall (opera house)

In 2004, the old hall was renamed after the Opera House's architect. The Utzon Hall is used to host a range of events, including musical performances.

Uses
The Opera House hosts opera, ballet, concerts, and theater in five halls. There are also rooms for conferences and meetings.

Construction
The Sydney Opera House was built in stages between 1959 and 1973. The original architect was Jorn Utzon, from Denmark.

233
The number of architects who submitted designs for the Opera House.

Auditorium
(concert hall)

New Colonnade

The new western colonnade opened in 2006. The new walkway is 148 feet long. It runs along the side of the building, allowing light to flood in and giving people visiting the Opera House views of Sydney Harbour.

The Concert Hall

This magnificent venue can hold 2679 concert-goers. It is the Opera House's largest interior venue, and is home to the Sydney Symphony Orchestra and the Australian Chamber Orchestra.

THE WORLD IN FIGURES INTRODUCTION

This atlas has looked at each continent in detail, examining the range of landscapes and the many different people who live in each region. The next chapter looks at the facts and figures behind many of the world's problems, from overpopulation and food sources to water shortages and energy resources. This chapter discusses how these problems affect the global economy.

FUEL
ENDLESS LINES OF FREIGHT CARRIERS FULL OF COAL ARE EXPORTED
TO COUNTRIES AROUND THE WORLD TO GENERATE ELECTRICITY.

CONTINENTS AND COUNTRIES

Humankind has made all kinds of divisions and boundaries that shape the world map politically. While many of the borders have names that have existed naturally, some have been formed as a result of historical events, such as war.

BORDERS
Usually shown as lines on a map, borders mark the geographic areas that define separate countries.

The Land Area

Most of the Earth's surface is covered in water. The land area, representing about one-third of the Earth, is divided into seven continents. Central America and the Caribbean is sometimes considered a subcontinent and is part of the continent of North America.

38
million

The number of times that the world's largest country, Russia, is greater than the Vatican City, the world's smallest country.

North America
9,388,232 sq mi

Central America and Caribbean
292,725 sq mi

Africa
11,688,432 sq mi

South America
6,899,725 sq mi

Antarctica
5,495,426 sq mi

Africa: **53**

Central America and the Caribbean: **21**

Oceania: **14**

North America: **3**

South America: **12**

Antarctica: **0**

Europe: **45**

Asia: **48**

MANY COUNTRIES

Each flag in the illustration on the right represents a country, colored to match the continent or subcontinent it belongs to. Antarctica is unique in having no individual countries.

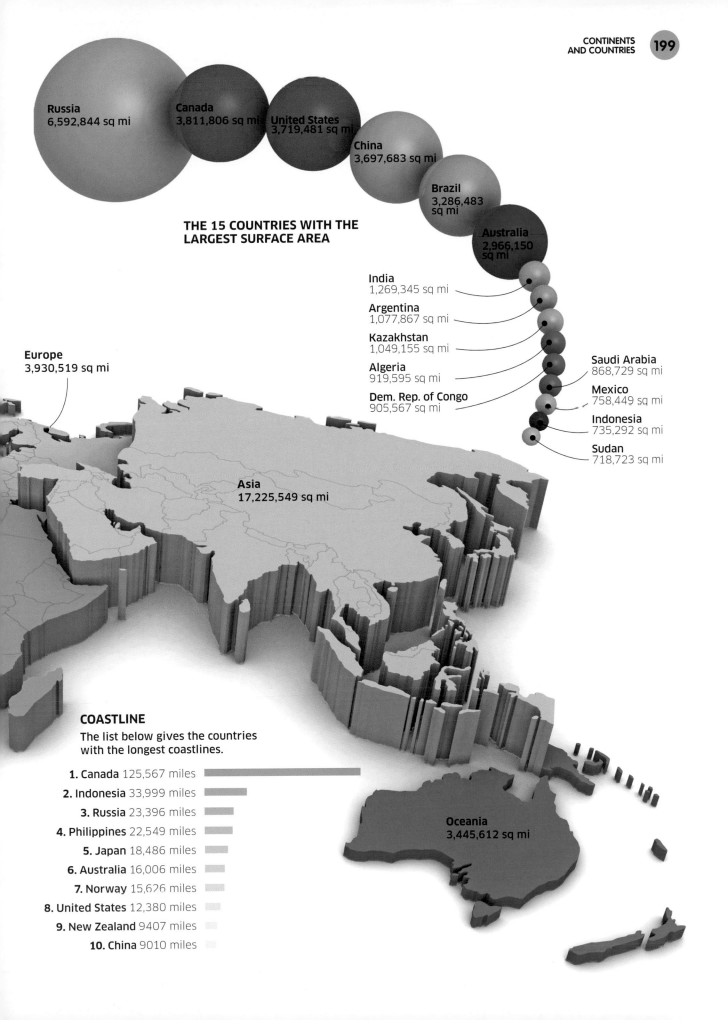

THE 15 COUNTRIES WITH THE LARGEST SURFACE AREA

Russia 6,592,844 sq mi

Canada 3,811,806 sq mi

United States 3,719,481 sq mi

China 3,697,683 sq mi

Brazil 3,286,483 sq mi

Australia 2,966,150 sq mi

India 1,269,345 sq mi

Argentina 1,077,867 sq mi

Kazakhstan 1,049,155 sq mi

Algeria 919,595 sq mi

Dem. Rep. of Congo 905,567 sq mi

Saudi Arabia 868,729 sq mi

Mexico 758,449 sq mi

Indonesia 735,292 sq mi

Sudan 718,723 sq mi

Europe 3,930,519 sq mi

Asia 17,225,549 sq mi

Oceania 3,445,612 sq mi

COASTLINE

The list below gives the countries with the longest coastlines.

1. Canada 125,567 miles
2. Indonesia 33,999 miles
3. Russia 23,396 miles
4. Philippines 22,549 miles
5. Japan 18,486 miles
6. Australia 16,006 miles
7. Norway 15,626 miles
8. United States 12,380 miles
9. New Zealand 9407 miles
10. China 9010 miles

CLIMATE ZONES

Different parts of the world can be divided into climate zones. These are regions where there is a similar temperature, atmospheric pressure, rainfall, and other precipitation and humidity.

CLIMATIC ZONES

- Rain forest
- Savanna
- Steppe
- Desert
- Humid temperate (dry season)
- Temperate humid
- Temperate
- Tundra
- Glacial
- Mountain climate
- Continental cool temperate
- Cool temperate continental
- Cold temperate continental

Ice Cap

HUDSON BAY

Rocky Mountains

Temperate

NORTH AMERICA

Appalachian Mountains

ATLANTIC OCEAN

CENTRAL AMERICA AND CARIBBEAN

Amazon Basin

Andes

SOUTH AMERICA

PACIFIC OCEAN

Pampas Region

Patagonia

Jungle

Temperate

The temperate climate has mild temperatures and moderate rainfall throughout the year. Winters are mild with long periods without frost. The temperate regions are ideal for most agricultural producers.

Tropical Climate

Tropical regions have high temperatures throughout the year, combined with heavy rains. About half of the world's population lives in tropical climates. Here, the vegetation is lush and there is a very high level of moisture caused by rainfall and plant transpiration.

Extreme Temperatures

The highest temperature was recorded in Libya in 1922: 136 °F. The lowest temperature was recorded in 1983 at Vostok Station, Antarctica (-128.6 °F). The area of Marble Bar in Western Australia has a constant high temperature. From October 7, 1923 to April 31, 1924, the temperature was never lower than 100 °F.

Nullagine
Newman

Marble Bar
Port Hedland
150 m

Cold Temperate

Very cold winters with frequent frosts are typical of these regions. Because the average temperature is so low, there is very little farming here and the landscape is mainly covered in natural vegetation.

Forests and lakes

Siberia

West Siberian Plains

ASIA

Tundra and taiga

North European Plains

EUROPE

Alps

Black Sea

Caspian Sea

Himalayas

MEDITERRANEAN SEA

Mountain Climate

At high altitudes, the climate is dominated by very low temperatures, high winds, and irregular and almost perpetual snow. There is no vegetation on the summits.

Arabian Peninsula

Sahara

Congo Basin

INDIAN OCEAN

ÁFRICA

OCEANIA

Gibson Desert

Temperatures and Winds

The temperatures on Earth depend on energy from the Sun. The temperature influences the atmospheric pressure of each zone, and these differences produce winds.

Desert

Desert

Desert regions receive almost no rain.

TORNADOES

On April 3 and 4, 1974, there were no fewer than 148 tornadoes in 18 hours.

OVERPOPULATION

As the world population continues to increase, the pressure to meet the basic needs of life will become greater. The differences between the standard of living of the most economically developed countries and the least developed countries will remain high, because the population will grow even more in poor countries.

Japan
Crowded streets in Tokyo.

DIFFERENT VALUES

Life Expectancy

This is the average number of years a person is expected to live. In Europe, during the time of the Roman Empire, the average life expectancy was 25 years. In 1900, it reached 50 across the world. Thanks to many advances in medicine, the average life expectancy now stands at 67 years. Nevertheless, there are big differences between the life expectancies of the rich and poor.

A World of Difference

Life expectancy in some countries:

COUNTRY	AGE
JAPAN	82
SWITZERLAND	81
UNITED STATES	78
ARGENTINA	75
VENEZUELA	73
MONGOLIA	67
NIGERIA	47

The Future

By 2050, the United Nations predicts that the population of the Earth will be 9.1 billion people.

Asia at the Head

East Asia has the highest concentration of people in the world.

Overcrowding
With nearly 17 million people in Calcutta, India, problems such as poverty, water pollution, traffic, and noise are common.

Solutions
Solutions to problems such as food, water, and energy shortages—and also poor healthcare and education—need to be found to support the ever-growing global population.

COUNTRIES WITH MOST PEOPLE
Two-thirds of the world population live in just 16 countries.

- 3.5% Indonesia
- 4.5% United States of America
- 18% India
- 19% China
- 55% Rest of the world

URBAN GEOGRAPHY

Huge City
A **conurbation** is the result of growth and expansion of a central city. Neighboring towns or cities that have developed are absorbed to form a single unit.

CONURBATIONS	PEOPLE
Tokyo, Japan	38,000,000
Guangzhou, China	24,500,000
Seoul, South Korea	24,200,000
Mexico City, Mexico	23,400,000
New Delhi, India	23,200,000

AGRICULTURE

The production of **genetically modified (GM) crops** is increasing. Scientists believe that genetic modification can improve crops, and reduce costs and the amount of chemicals used. Some environmentalists warn that not enough is known about the effect of GM crops on the environment and on consumers.

NO LIMITS
The production of GM crops has affected both industrialized and developing countries.

Countries with GM Crops

This map shows the distribution of GM crops in 2010, in millions of acres.

PERCENTAGE OF FARMED LAND IN ARGENTINA

54%
GM crops (soy, corn, and cotton)

46%
Natural crops

NATURAL AND GM SOY AND COTTON CROPS AROUND THE WORLD

Soy

24%
Natural

76%
GM

Cotton

62%
GM

38%
Natural

Canada 22

France 0.1
Spain 0.25
Portugal 0.

United States 165

Mexico 0.25

Honduras 0.12

ATLANTIC OCEAN

Colombia 0.12

Bolivia 2.2

Paraguay

Chile 0.12

Brazil 63

Uruguay 2.7

PACIFIC OCEAN

Argentina 57

90

The percentage of all GM crops produced in Argentina, Brazil, the United States, and Canada.

TOP PRODUCERS OF WHEAT
In millions of tons per year

1. China 112
2. India 79
3. USA 68
4. Russia 64
5. France 39
6. Canada 29
7. Germany 26
8. Ukraine 26
9. Australia 21
10. Pakistan 21

TOP PRODUCERS OF POTATOES
In millions of tons per year

1. China 72
2. Russia 36
3. India 26
4. USA 20
5. Ukraine 19
6. Poland 11
7. Germany 11
8. Belarus 8
9. Netherlands 7
10. France 6

Germany 0.12

Poland 0.12

Romania 0.12

Slovakia 0.12

Czech Republic 0.12

China 9.4

India 23.3

Philippines 0.12

INDIAN OCEAN

Australia 1.7

5.4 South Africa

KEY
BIOTECH CROPS

Corn Carnation Rape Tomato Soy Cotton

Poplar Petunia Alfalfa Pumpkin Papaya Pepper

Less Carbon Dioxide
GM crops use fewer chemicals and so emit less carbon dioxide. Reducing carbon dioxide (a greenhouse gas) in the atmosphere means that the greenhouse effect has less impact.

FISHING

In its global report on fishing, the Food and Agriculture Organization of the United Nations (FAO) stated that 19 percent of fishing resources are overexploited and 8 percent are depleted. Although the situation has remained stable since 2000, overfishing will ultimately have a serious impact on the world's food supply.

All at Sea

The seas and oceans provide 90 percent of fish that is caught. The remaining 10 percent come from freshwater sources. The environmental charity Greenpeace has called for a law to protect 40 percent of the oceans from overfishing.

Hungry Oceans

Due to the overfishing of anchovy and mackerel, natural predators of these fish are left with a decreasing source of food. This has affected both dolphins and tuna.

Shrimp Farming

The world shrimp production has stabilized as a result of shrimp farming. India, China, the United States, Thailand, Indonesia, Mexico, Malaysia, Japan, Vietnam, and Brazil are the leading countries engaged in shrimp farming.

MAJOR EXPORTERS (2008)

These are the annual figures of the top fish-exporting countries, in billions of dollars.

1. China 10.1
2. Norway 6.9
3. Thailand 6.5
4. Denmark 4.6
5. Vietnam 4.5
6. USA 4.5

Work

Fishing is very important to the livelihoods of millions of people around the world. More than 60 million people are said to work in the fishing industry, and half of this workforce are women.

SOURCE OF PROTEIN

Important Values

Fish and fish products make up 15 percent of the animal protein eaten by half of the global population. This means that on average, each person eats about 37 pounds of fish each year.

LIVESTOCK

Livestock is an important resource and a good indicator of the economy of a country. It is is used for meat and other products, such as leather and wool. In less economically developed countries, animals are also used to move agricultural equipment and as a means of transportation.

DEFORESTATION
Around 80 percent of the Brazilian Amazon Rain Forest has been deforested to raise cattle.

PROTECTION
HEALTH

Health Problems

According to the FAO, the risk of disease being transmitted from animals to humans has increased because more animals are being reared. Influenza A is one such disease.

Dairy Producers

The graph below shows the major dairy producers. Consumption of dairy products varies widely around the world. It depends on the eating habits and diet of the population as well as its wealth.

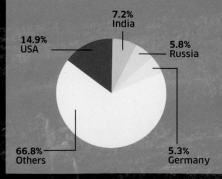

7.2%
India

14.9%
USA

5.8%
Russia

66.8%
Others

5.3%
Germany

Meat Producers

There are about 1.3 billion cattle in the world. Countries such as the United States, Brazil, and China have large areas of fertile land for raising cattle.

Poultry

According to the FAO, in the last decade, the consumption of poultry products in less economically developed countries increased each year by 5.8 percent.

POULTRY PRODUCTION (in thousands of tons)

1. USA 19,691
2. China 15,052
3. Brazil 9225
4. Mexico 2585
5. India 2313

Meat Production

As the global population grows, there is an increase in the demand for meat products in less economically developed countries. The FAO reports that meat production will grow from 278 million tons a year to 463 million tons by 2050.

CHANGING STATISTICS

World Meat Consumption

The protein intake from eating meat has changed over time. In 1968, the global average of proteins from meat per person per day was 0.3 oz. In 1998, this had increased to 0.4 oz.

MEATS CONSUMED

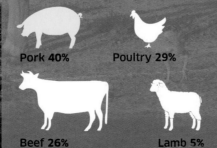

Pork 40% Poultry 29%

Beef 26% Lamb 5%

PER PERSON PER DAY

PLACE	OUNCES
Developed countries	7.9
Latin America	5.2
Far East and South Asia	4.0
Middle East	1.5
Developing countries	1.7
Africa	1.1

A THIRSTY WORLD

According to the World Health Organization, about 900 million people worldwide lack access to safe drinking water. Another 2.5 billion, over a third of the world's population, lack adequate sanitation systems. In some countries, water is so scarce that not a drop is wasted: the water used to wash a baby is then used for washing clothes or cleaning the kitchen.

RIGHTS
Environmental organizations believe that water is not a commodity but a basic human right.

Human Water Consumption

This map shows that the water intended for human consumption is much less than that used in agriculture and industry.

MAJOR CONSUMERS OF WATER

- Industrial use
- Industrial and agricultural use
- Industrial use, with important domestic use
- Domestic use
- Domestic and agricultural use
- Agricultural use, but with important domestic use
- Agricultural use
- Agricultural use, with important industrial use
- Agricultural use, with less important industrial use
- No data

Water Shortages

In many African countries, people have to line up each day to get water. Every year, 1.5 million children die from diarrhea and dehydration, which could have been prevented by having access to clean drinking water.

Human Health

It is estimated that to ensure a person's basic needs, such as washing, sanitation, drinking, and cooking, each person needs 5–13 gallons of clean, uncontaminated water each day.

13

The percentage of people living in Afghanistan who have access to safe drinking water.

Role of Women

Women play a key role in domestic water use, because they are often responsible for cooking, looking after children, and washing dishes, clothes, and the house. In places where there is no running water, it is often the women in the area who walk to fetch water. However, women are often left out of decisions on the planning and management of water resources.

OIL

The world's richest countries depend on oil as their main source of energy. However, we know that oil reserves are running out. As a result, the price of oil has gone up and this has affected the global economy.

Map of Oil Consumption and Production

This map shows the largest users and producers of oil. In red is the amount used each day, while blue shows the amount produced each day. The figures are the amount used or produced per day in millions of barrels (one barrel is equivalent to 42 gallons of oil).

The biggest users
The world uses about 85 million barrels of oil every day. The biggest user is the United States.

The biggest producers
Saudi Arabia, Russia, and the United States are the biggest oil producers.

■ Main shipping routes
■ Alternative shipping routes

70

The percentage of oil consumed in the United States that is used as fuel for transportation.

LESS OIL
Supplies of oil and natural gas (also found in oil fields) are going to become smaller over the next decade.

Canada
2264 3288

USA
20,687

8330

Mexico
1997 3707

ATLANTIC OCEAN

PACIFIC OCEAN

Venezuela
2803

Brazil
2217

USES OF OIL

Fuel
About 95 percent of the world's vehicles use fuels made from oil. As a result, the cost of transporting goods goes up when the price of oil goes up.

Making Electricity
Much of the world's electricity is made in power plants using oil or gas as fuel. These power plants need to be replaced with plants that use other sources of energy.

Rising Oil Prices

Possible causes for the rise in the price of oil:
1. There has been a rise in demand for oil in growing economies, such as India and China.

2. The amount of oil left in current oil fields is falling, and those who consume the oil have as yet to find a new source.

Norway
2786

Russia
2811
9677

United Kingdom
1830

Germany
2665

Japan
5159

France
1961

Italy
1732

China
7201   3865

South Korea
2174

Iraq
2008

Iran
1686   4148

Algeria
2122

Kuwait 2675

PACIFIC OCEAN

Saudi Arabia
2443   10,665

United Arab Emirates
2675

Nigeria
2443

India
2675

INDIAN OCEAN

4000

The number of ships used to transport 43 million barrels of oil every day.

Plastics

Many goods are made of plastic, which is a material made partly from oil. Scientists are now looking for other materials to use instead of plastics.

Other Uses

Oil is used to make many things, including dyes, fertilizer, and asphalt (left, used in building roads). An increase in the price of oil affects a huge number of the things that we use.

LIGHTING THE PLANET

Seen from space, the Earth is well lit by electricity. The generation of electricity by burning fossil fuels (coal, oil, and gas) has serious environmental implications. As a result, new technologies are being tested and alternative sources of energy are being sought.

NO STARS
In many cities, stars cannot be seen in the night due to the reflection of electric lights.

Planet of Night Light

At nightfall, in many urban settings, the sunlight is replaced by electrical lighting until the Sun rises again.

London, UK

París, France

Madrid, Spain

New York, USA

Los Angeles, USA

Miami, USA

Caracas, Venezuela

CREATING ELECTRICITY

Electricity has to be generated. To do this, different sources are used. Most of these sources, such as coal, oil, and gas, cause high levels of pollution and/or increased carbon dioxide (CO_2) emissions.

Oil (5.8%)
Accounts for 38 percent of CO_2 emissions into the atmosphere.

Other (2.3%)
These are clean and **renewable energies,** such as solar, wind, geothermal, and biomass.

Nuclear (14.8%)
Clean and virtually renewable but has the problem of radioactive waste and possible accidents.

Coal (41%)
The most polluting of all power sources and is responsible for 42 percent of the CO_2 emissions into the atmosphere.

Río de Janeiro, Brazil

Sao Paulo, Brazil

Buenos Aires, Argentina

Hydroelectric (16%)
It is clean and renewable but damming rivers causes ecological problems and displacement of humans.

Gas (20.1%)
It accounts for 19 percent of CO_2 emissions into the atmosphere.

65

The percentage of humans who live under electrically lit skies.

Light Pollution

Electric lighting has been one of the most remarkable human inventions. However, electric lights also cause massive pollution.

Correct **Incorrect**

Increasing

This drawing shows how artificial lighting can be used effectively to reduce the pollution it creates.

Moscow, Russia

Beijing, China

Rome, Italy

Tokyo, Japan

Seoul, South Korea

Taipei, Taiwan

Mumbai, India

Hong Kong, China

Bangkok, Thailand

New Delhi, India

MAJOR PRODUCERS

The terawatt per hour (TWh) is used to measure large amounts of electrical energy and is equivalent to one billion watts.

1. USA 22.6%
2. China 15.2%
3. Japan 5.8%
4. Russia 5.3%
5. India 3.9%
6. Germany 3.3%
7. Canada 3.2%
8. France 3%
9. Brazil 2.2%
10. South Korea 2.1%

Johannesburg, South Africa

Sydney, Australia

The United States consumes nearly one-third of the world production of electricity from nuclear sources. France and Japan are major producers of this type of energy.

MAKING CONNECTIONS

According to recent research, one in four people on Earth use the Internet. This new reality has accelerated to unprecedented levels the process of globalization that is facing our world.

FACEBOOK
In 2010, according to IWS (see below), the total number of Facebook users was estimated to be 517,760,460.

Radiography of the Network

On average, 32 percent of the world's population has Internet access. However, this is not uniform and the most populous countries, with a certain level of development, have the highest access.

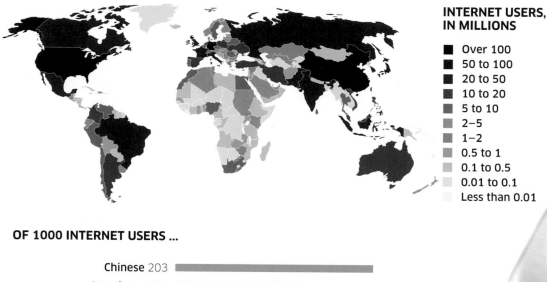

INTERNET USERS, IN MILLIONS

- Over 100
- 50 to 100
- 20 to 50
- 10 to 20
- 5 to 10
- 2–5
- 1–2
- 0.5 to 1
- 0.1 to 0.5
- 0.01 to 0.1
- Less than 0.01

OF 1000 INTERNET USERS ...

Nationality	Count
Chinese	203
Americans	144
Japanese	56
Indians	49
Brazilians	40
Germans	33
French	25
Russians	23
Koreans	22
Other nationalities	405

2011
According to Internet World Stats (IWS), there were over 2 billion Internet users.

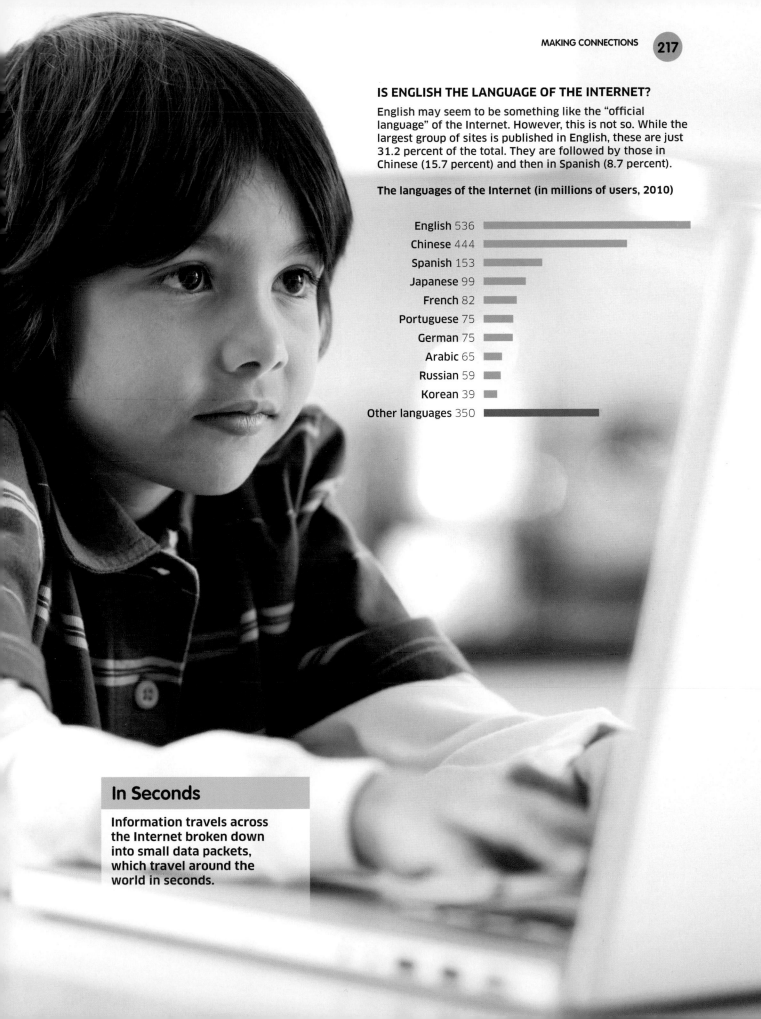

IS ENGLISH THE LANGUAGE OF THE INTERNET?

English may seem to be something like the "official language" of the Internet. However, this is not so. While the largest group of sites is published in English, these are just 31.2 percent of the total. They are followed by those in Chinese (15.7 percent) and then in Spanish (8.7 percent).

The languages of the Internet (in millions of users, 2010)

Language	Users
English	536
Chinese	444
Spanish	153
Japanese	99
French	82
Portuguese	75
German	75
Arabic	65
Russian	59
Korean	39
Other languages	350

In Seconds

Information travels across the Internet broken down into small data packets, which travel around the world in seconds.

GLOSSARY

ACOUSTICS
The properties or qualities of a room or building that determine how sound is transmitted in it.

ADAPTATIONS
Changes to animals and plants over a long period of time to ensure their survival in a specific biome. For example, animals found at the Poles usually have very thick coats.

AMPHITHEATER
An open, circular, or oval building, with levels of seating around a central space, used for events such as drama or sports.

ANCESTORS
People from whom another person is descended.

ANIMISM
A religious belief that everything on Earth is imbued with a spirit.

ANTHROPOLOGISTS
People who study and compare human societies and cultures.

ASTRONOMICAL CLOCK
A clock that shows the positions of the Sun, Moon, planets, and large constellations of stars.

AVALANCHES
Large bodies of snow, ice, and rocks falling rapidly down a mountainside.

BAUXITE
A clayey rock from which aluminum is mined.

BIODIVERSITY
The variety of plant and animal life in a particular place.

CARBON DIOXIDE
A colorless gas found in the atmosphere, which is given off when humans breathe out.

CARGO
Goods carried on a ship, airplane, or in a motor vehicle.

CARNIVOROUS
Describes animals that eat only meat.

CONTINENTAL DRIFT
The gradual movement of the continents across the Earth's surface.

CONURBATION
A large urban area in which several towns merge with the suburbs of a central city.

COSMOPOLITAN
Describes something, such as a city, with many different people and cultures.

CREMATE
To burn a dead person's body.

DEHYDRATION
When the body loses a lot of water. Dehydration can cause a dry, sticky mouth, sleepiness, and can lead to vomiting and death.

ELEVATION
The height of a mountain.

EROSION
The gradual wearing away of something by water, wind, or ice.

EUROPEAN UNION (EU)
An economic and political union of 27 countries within Europe.

EXPEDITION
A journey undertaken by a team or group of people to discover and explore a new place.

EXTINCT
Describes a plant or animal that no longer survives. For example, the Arctic reindeer is extinct.

FAUNA
Animals.

FERTILE
Land of a quality on which crops can be grown.

FLORA
Plants.

FOLD MOUNTAINS
Mountains that are formed when two tectonic plates are pushed together.

FOSSIL
Describes something that has become preserved in rock, or fossilized.

GENETICALLY MODIFIED
Describes something that has been changed by scientists to produce certain characteristics. For example, animals can be injected with hormones to produce more meat.

GLACIER
A slowly moving mass or river of ice.

HEATWAVE
Abnormally hot weather for a long period of time.

HERBIVORES
Animals, such as elephants and giraffes, that eat only plants.

HIV
Short for the human immunodeficiency virus. This is the virus that causes AIDS, an illness that can be fatal.

HUNTER-GATHERER
A person who lives by hunting, fishing, and harvesting wild food.

ICE CAP
A covering of ice over a large area, usually at the Poles.

ICEBERG
A large floating piece of ice that has been carried out to sea.

IMMIGRANTS
People from a different country.

IMPORT
To bring goods into a country.

INDUSTRIALIZE
To develop industries on a large scale.

INSCRIPTIONS
Something "written" on a monument.

LAVA
Hot molten or semifluid rock that has erupted from a volcano.

LIMESTONE
A hard rock used in building.

LUNAR CALENDAR
A calendar based on the phases of the Moon.

MARSUPIAL
A mammal, usually found in Australia, whose young are carried in a pouch on the mother's belly.

MAUSOLEUM
A large building that houses a tomb or several tombs.

MIGRATE
To move from one country or region to another.

MUDSLIDES
A mass of mud that has fallen down a hillside or other slope.

NICKEL
A silvery-white metal.

NOCTURNAL
Describes animals, such as owls, that are active mainly at night.

NOMADIC
Describes people that travel from place to place.

NUCLEAR POWER
Electricity generated from a nuclear reactor.

OTTOMAN EMPIRE
A Turkish empire that lasted from the end of the thirteenth century to the beginning of the twentieth century.

OUTBACK
The inland areas of Australia where very few people live.

OZONE LAYER
A layer of gases around the Earth that absorbs most of the radiation reaching the Earth from the Sun.

PADDIES
Fields where rice is grown.

PAPYRUS
A water plant used in ancient Egypt to make paper.

PERMAFROST
A thick layer of soil that remains frozen throughout the year.

PHARAOH
A ruler of ancient Egypt.

PLATEAU
A flat area of land that is usually at a high altitude.

PLATINUM
A precious silvery-white metal.

POLYTHEISM
The belief in or worship of more than one god.

RENAISSANCE
The growth of European art and literature from the fourteenth to the sixteenth century.

RENEWABLE ENERGY
Energy from a source that will not run out, such as the Sun.

SARCOPHAGUS
A stone coffin.

SCANDINAVIAN
Describes someone or something from Scandinavia (Norway, Sweden, and Denmark).

SCAVENGERS
Animals, such as hyenas, that feed on dead animals, plant material, or refuse.

SOLAR POWER
Electricity generated by harnessing the Sun's energy.

SYMMETRICAL
Describes something made up of exactly the same parts facing each other.

TECTONIC PLATES
Pieces of the Earth's crust and upper mantle.

TERRACED GARDEN
A garden that has steps or raised areas.

TITANIUM
A hard silver-gray metal.

TRIBUTARY
A river or stream flowing into a larger river or lake.

TROPICAL STORM
A storm that has thunderstorms, very strong winds, and brings with it heavy rain.

URANIUM
A silvery-white metal, used to create nuclear power.

URBANIZATION
The process whereby a place becomes more urban or city-like.

VIADUCT
A bridge made up of several small spans.

INDEX